ORGANS
for AMERICA

THE LIFE AND WORK OF
DAVID TANNENBERG

by William H. Armstrong

Philadelphia   1967
University of Pennsylvania Press

7554

Printed in the United States of America

To my wife, Gloria,
and her father, Lester Cassler,
direct descendants of
David Tannenberg
through his daughter
Anna Rosina Tannenberg Cassler

FOREWORD

David Tannenberg was one of many immigrants from Central Europe who came to the New World in the mid-1700s in search of opportunity and religious freedom. His trade was that of a cabinetmaker and housebuilder, but the stuff of genius was in him. The manner in which his life developed in the early Moravian communities, how the artisan evolved into the artist, and how Tannenberg came to build instruments that still exemplify for us today the best of the organ maker's art, is the theme of this book. William Armstrong has transformed a mountain of painstaking research into a human and entertaining document.

Tannenberg had no training as organ builder in Europe. His only instruction appears to have come from an older Pennsylvania organ builder, Johann Gottlob Klemm. Klemm, however, could have given him only the rudiments of the art. The rest Tannenberg taught himself, guided by a sensitive ear and the skill of a fine craftsman.

It seems always the lot of an artist to experience opposition. In those pre-Revolutionary days, elders of the Moravian Church held a tight rein over every detail of community life. As Mr. Armstrong tells the story, it must hardly have been possible to drive a nail in a board without permission. The Moravian fathers sought at first to restrain Tannenberg in his organ-building aspirations, on the basis that it "would take him out into the world too much." Reprimands for what seem to us the slightest of offenses, such as allowing his son to buy a pocket watch, were often Tannenberg's lot. But despite all problems, Tannenberg's relations with the "City Fathers" remained always cordial, and it was the Moravian Church which gave him his lifelong opportunity.

In Tannenberg's development, one notes the tenacity of the true artist, an attitude strengthened by deep religious conviction. He never lacked work. He built progressively larger organs for cities as far away as Philadelphia, Albany, and Frederick, Maryland. George Washington, John Hancock, John Adams, Benjamin Franklin were among the notables who listened to his instruments.

Tannenberg never revisited Europe nor did he travel within the Colonies to learn from other organ builders. He neither had nor did he need the spur of competitors. His art seemed preformed in his mind, and his natural ear governed his craftsmanship.

What would Tannenberg's life have been, had he remained in Europe? His innate skill could well have put him alongside Arp Schnitger and the two Silbermanns, Gottfried and Andreas. But one may hazard a guess that already-established builders would have presented insurmountable competition, and that Tannenberg might have had to stick to his carpentry trade. Tannenberg came to America for opportunity, and he found it. His life is thus a part of early Americana, and while in adventure it hardly compares with the experiences of General John Sutter, of California Gold Rush fame (Sutter also eventually settled in Tannenberg's adopted town of Lititz), the organs are a tangible and continuing legacy.

Why write a book about an organ builder and a few old church organs? "What is the true measure of Tannenberg's work?"—to use Mr. Armstrong's words. The answer involves music history, organ design, Benjamin Franklin and his kite, and —on the part of the reader—a willingness to listen and discern between fine and merely indifferent musical tone.

In Tannenberg's day organs were built the way they had been for a thousand years. The pumper pumped, the player played, and the organist's fingers were extended, almost literally, by means of "trackers," mechanical linkage to open the pipe valves beneath the pipes. It was a simple method, and extremely efficient.

Along came Benjamin Franklin and many inventive, but not

always musical, minds. Electricity was harnessed and put to work in the organ. The perfection of simplicity was lost. It's fine, of course, to have a non-tireable electric blower for a pumper, but it's not fine at all to have one's finger effort intercepted by an electric magnet or a pneumatic.

Tannenberg's method afforded the player a degree of "touch," to the extent that it is possible to inflect pipe speech. But a magnet is a robot—red or green, stop or go, on or off, in short, with no intermediate control. Once magnets and pneumatics are added to organ playing action, subtleties of accent and phrasing go by the board.

Perhaps you will say, "But isn't it just the pipes that give the tone?" The answer is yes and no. Tone does originate in pipes, but this tone is greatly affected and often ruined by the playing action, as well as by other factors in organ design. There is, in fact, a great gulf fixed between the buoyant and elegant tones obtainable from pipes in a well-designed organ, encased (but not enclosed), on low wind pressure, with a well-adjusted and controllable tracker playing action, and the harsh, inflexible accents that usually come from an organ under the arbitrary command of electricity. Centuries of organ building appear to prove that fine tone is obtainable only through such methods as Tannenberg knew.

In thought, and in decisions about a new organ or the rebuilding of an old organ, many an individual will find himself on the great divide, having to weigh the merits of the old and the new— that is, "tracker" versus electric playing action. For the community, and for a good many years, a lot depends on the wisdom of this choice. Tannenberg has the answer, an answer as valid today as it was in his time.

It would be wonderful if Tannenberg's larger instruments, such as the one in Philadelphia, could have survived. We would undoubtedly find them the equal of anything built in Europe. The smaller instruments that we have are fully comparable in tonal quality, if not in size, to the best European organs.

Mr. Armstrong gives well-deserved credit to Albert Schweitzer, whose perceptive writings of some sixty years ago served so much to provoke today's interest in and question about organs. Schweitzer came up with the idea that "off with the old, on with the new" was not necessarily the best principle. In the case of organ building, Schweitzer said, the old was rather better. He insisted that older organs be preserved and treasured, and emulated in our building today. Naturally, Schweitzer was thinking of Europe, but he would have been equally delighted with Tannenberg's instruments. One wishes that the Doctor, on his one visit to the United States in 1949, could have seen and played the magnificent Tannenberg organ now in the Museum of the Historical Society of York County, York, Pennsylvania. This instrument, Tannenberg's last "opus," which I have had the privilege to play both in concert and for recordings, has lived throughout most of two centuries and bids fair to sound forth forever.

E. POWER BIGGS

PREFACE

At eleven o'clock on January 8, 1791, the President of the United States, accompanied by "his lady" and members of the Congress and the Pennsylvania Assembly, attended an organ concert at Zion Lutheran Church in Philadelphia.[1] Several months before when the President had attended a preview of the church's new organ, he had been welcomed by the anxious German pastor with several original English verses:

> Hail, Welcome Chief, him welcome here
> We love thee as our Father
> The very heart exults in thee
> And beats thy Name with Gladness
> O Washington, Our Washington
> Thou art Columbia's Honor
> Live long and still live happy.

One can be fairly certain that Washington did not return to Zion Church to hear more of Pastor Helmuth's poetry; it was the magnificent new pipe organ, the pride of the young capital city, which brought him back. With thirty-four stops and nearly two thousand speaking pipes, its 27-foot height adorned with glistening metal pipes and visions of sun and clouds, eagles and angels, there was no musical instrument in the new world to compare with it. In fact, as an overawed newspaper reporter boasted, many of the largest cities in Europe could not claim such an organ. But what was most a matter of pride was that the organ had been built by an American.

> This great and beautiful creation is the work of Mr. David Tanneberg, of Lititz in Lancaster County, who began to build organs here in America by his own instincts, but through reading, reflection and unwearied industry has raised

himself to such a height that if the most skilled European
builder should come here and examine this work, in the judgment of experts, he could only bestow praise and be won to
him.[2]

This book is the story of David Tannenberg, the organ
builder of Lititz, and of his organs. One of America's first full-
time organ builders, Tannenberg built or helped to build almost
fifty pipe organs for churches and individuals in six states, preparing them for such distant cities as Albany, New York, and
Salem, North Carolina. They were built not only for the use of
the Moravian Brethren, of which he was a member, but for
German Reformed and Lutheran churches as well and, in at
least one case, for a Roman Catholic church. The quality of
Tannenberg's work was such that he is recognized today as one of
the master organ builders, to be ranked alongside the Silbermanns
and Arp Schnitger in Europe.

In recent years a renewed interest in the old, mechanical,
"tracker action" organs has led to the rediscovery and restoration of most of Tannenberg's surviving works. But the story of
his life has never adequately been told, nor the measure of his
work been taken. The life and work of the master builder have
lain buried in the German manuscripts of the Moravian Brethren.
Contained in their pages is the fascinating story of a people rich
in music and religious devotion. It is from these pages that the
story of the one whom they proudly called Brother David
Tannenberg is taken.

Many people have helped in the preparation of this book.
I am most grateful to them for their patience with me when I
repeatedly sought their help in finding the sources for Tannenberg's life, for many efforts to open rusted church safes, and to
locate faded documents long untouched. I am especially grateful
to Dr. Theodore G. Tappert, who first encouraged me in this
study, to the Moravian Archives in Winston-Salem for making
available their Tannenberg materials (now in the archives of the
Moravian Music Foundation), and to the Rev. Vernon Nelson
for his willingness to open the Archives of the Moravian Church

in Bethlehem, Pennsylvania, to me and to help me locate and interpret the rich sources there. I also appreciate the help of those persons who read the manuscript of the book and offered suggestions concerning it: Vernon Nelson, Barbara Owen, E. Power Biggs, and Marion M. Meyer. Miss Meyer has also provided invaluable assistance to me in the preparation of the manuscript for publication.

One day last year, after long days away from my family, studying the organs and their builder, my daughter asked, "What's so important about Tannenberg anyway?" I hope that when she is old enough to read this she will find the answer here.

WILLIAM H. ARMSTRONG

A NOTE ON THE NAME TANNENBERG

There has been some confusion over the name of the organ builder, some referring to him as Tannenberg, others as Tanneberger. Actually, as anyone who has leafed through old documents can testify, consistent spelling of names has only recently been counted a virtue and the variations of a name can be legion. Thus the organ builder appears as Tanneberg, Danneberg, Donnaberger, Donebarger, Tannelberger, Fanneberg, and still others. But the two forms which appear with regularity are Tanneberger and Tannenberg.

The family was known among Moravians as Tanneberger, and almost always, throughout his life, the organ builder was referred to by others as Tanneberger. The builder himself, however, adopted the form Tannenberg and used it rather consistently, especially in his later years. In spite of his inability to convince his contemporaries to use that form, it seems only just that we should refer to him by the name he preferred.

CONTENTS

ILLUSTRATIONS

PART I
DAVID TANNENBERG

1

From Berthelsdorf to Bethlehem

The story of David Tannenberg must also be the story of the Moravian Church. Tannenberg thought of himself first, not as a German or an American, or even as an organ builder. He was first of all a member of the religious community properly called the *Unitas Fratrum* (Unity of the Brethren) but more commonly, Moravians. To say that Tannenberg was a Moravian is to say much more than that William McKinley was a Methodist, or even that Henry Ward Beecher was a Congregationalist. Tannenberg's membership in the *Unitas Fratrum* committed him to life in a closed Christian community, played a major part in his choice of a vocation and even of a wife, involved him in a rich tradition of worship, music, and education, and brought him into intimate contact with a Christian tradition reaching back to the year 1415.

On July 6, 1415, John Hus was burned at the stake at Constance, Baden, Germany, for his supposed heresies in opposing the teaching of the Catholic Church. Hus was a Czech, the rector of the University of Prague, and after his death his followers in Bohemia carried on his cause. In 1457, at the village of Kunwald, near the castle of Lititz in Bohemia, the group organized themselves as the *Unitas Fratrum*. Severely persecuted at first, the society grew strong in Bohemia, Moravia, and Poland after the Protestant Reformation, only to be all but obliterated in the wars of the Counter-Reformation. For a century the group was alive only as a "hidden seed," a tradition and an episcopacy passed

3

on secretly from one generation to another, under the constant threat of the Catholic Church. Then in 1722 the society experienced a rebirth when some of the strongest families fled Moravia, going for refuge to nearby Saxony and finding it on the estates of a young Lutheran count, Nicolaus Ludwig von Zinzendorf. It was under the leadership and protection of this man, "the Count and Lord of Zinzendorf, Lord of the Baronies of Freydeck, Schoeneck, Thuernstein and the Vale of Wachovia, Lord of the Manor, upper, middle and lower Berthelsdorf, Hereditary Warden of the Chase to his Imperial Majesty in the Duchy of Austria below Ems, late Aulic and Justicial Counsellor to His Majesty, Augustus of Poland, for the Electorate of Saxony,"[1] that the Moravian Brethren began to flourish. And it was at Berthelsdorf, on the estates of Count Zinzendorf, that David Tannenberg was born on March 21, 1728, of parents who only the year before had fled from Zauchtenthal, Moravia, to the safety of Saxony.

"In the eastern part of Moravia [now Czechoslovakia], where the Oder takes its rise, and the pastures are so luxuriant that the peasantry term the country *Kuhländl,* or kine-land, there lies, in a beautiful valley enclosed by the spurs of the Middle Carpathians, a small village named Zauchtenthal."[2] Here both of Tannenberg's parents were born as were, indeed, not a few of the earliest leaders of the renewed society of the Brethren. His father, Johann Tanneberger, son of David Tanneberger and his wife Dorothea (Gross), was born on September 21, 1693.[3] The family was among those who participated in secret gatherings of the "awakened" for services of song and prayer. In his earliest days Johann enjoyed these gatherings and longed to know the Savior whom they worshiped, but as he later expressed it, "I began to be fond of the world, looked for and found bad company, and passed seven or eight years in corruption." In his twenty-seventh year his father died. (He had become sick and upon awaking one morning had said to his wife, "Do you know that I must bid farewell to you today?" and shortly thereafter sat down and died.) With that Johann returned home and took up his father's affairs. In 1721 he married Judith Nitschmann, who had been born in Zauchtenthal in 1698, the daughter of Heinrich Nitschmann.

A new interest in religion was aroused in Johann Tanneberger during the next years, especially by the visit of Christian David, whom John Wesley called "the Godly Carpenter,"[4] one of the zealous founders of the renewed church. Shortly thereafter, in 1724, five prominent churchmen fled to Saxony and Tanneberger came under suspicion in connection with their flight. Although he had known nothing of the flight, he was imprisoned for eight days, forced to sit "up under the roof," questioned daily, suffering from the cold, and receiving nothing to eat except what his friends secretly brought to him. When it became apparent that he had no information, he was released, but when others fled the land he was again arrested and placed in a filthy prison under cruel conditions. At times he was made to push wheelbarrows while chained to another prisoner; at other times he was forced to work with a block fastened to his leg. After some months he was released; then one evening it was announced that the next day the Brethren must renounce their teaching. That evening in July, 1726, Johann Tanneberger made the decision to flee with his wife and his year-and-a-half-old son. Although his wife was not in sympathy with her husband's religious convictions and would have preferred to stay in Moravia, the family left quietly the same night in a company of twelve persons. Traveling mostly by night, and with the assistance of various friends who guided them to other friendly homes, they finally arrived in September at Herrnhut, the Moravian village on Count Zinzendorf's estates.

Their joy at reaching Herrnhut was short-lived, however, for the village was still in the process of being built and was overcrowded from the growing number of refugees. Finding no work, the family removed early in 1727 to Berthelsdorf, about a mile away, rented a home for two years in the hope of returning to Herrnhut when there would be work available, but finally built a small house in Berthelsdorf and settled there permanently.

Tanneberger's wife, who previously had not participated in the religious activities, now became interested in the Bible studies of Pastor Johann Andreas Rothe,[5] or perhaps in the good pastor himself, for she became so attached to him that, when he left Berthelsdorf in 1737, she thought that Herrnhut and everything good would pass away, and seriously considered leaving with him. Fortunately, a dream convinced her that the community would survive his leaving and she was drawn closer to the Savior, finally being received into the congregation in 1743.

Desiring to be readmitted to the community in Herrnhut, the couple returned there in 1746 and became a part of that congregation. Here they lived until their deaths. Judith Tanneberger died on December 9, 1756, while Johann lived on in the Widower House, working at his trade of boot- and shoe-making until his death on October 21, 1770.

It was at Berthelsdorf, just a year after his parents' arrival, that David Tannenberg was born, the second son among eight children.[6] His parents' account of their flight from Moravia reads like an oft-told tale, and young David was undoubtedly well-informed about the providential nature of the family's deliverance. He could also testify that from childhood he had personally been directed to the Savior and had felt his attraction. These religious inclinations were heightened by the influence of Brother Biegel, the schoolmaster in Berthelsdorf, but the compelling influence was that of Count Zinzendorf himself. A chance encounter with the Count on the Hutberg (Mount of Protection) marked a turning point both in Tannenberg's religious life and in his education. He later related the incident in his memoir or autobiography.

> Once I found myself all alone on the Hutberg, where I was watching cattle and before I knew it the blessed Count Zinzendorf came right up to me and asked me who I belonged to and wrote it down, which disturbed me greatly. He arranged it so that on July 12, 1738, I was brought by my father's brother, Martin Tannenberg, into the children's school at the Wetterau in which the Savior manifested himself especially in my heart.

The meeting of the shepherd boy and the Count was too similar to the Old Testament stories of God's visitations to be taken lightly and it resulted in a deep attachment to the Count and to his people. The encounter also made it possible for Tannenberg to study for four years in the Wetterau, the region north of Frankfurt am Main where Zinzendorf had taken refuge during an exile from Saxony. There Tannenberg attended schools in various Moravian communities, first at the Ronneburg, then later at Marienborn and Herrnhaag.

During this period Count Zinzendorf planned a trip to Geneva with his son Christian Renatus to see whether the son might profitably study there. Zinzendorf also wanted to visit Calvin's Church in Geneva to present the Moravian message there. He took with him forty or fifty Moravian Brethren as his "Pilgrim Congregation." Among them was young David Tannenberg and, as he put it, some of his "playmates." The Count left for Geneva on January 24, 1741, with the youngsters following later with Brother Jacob Till, the whole group gathering at Geneva in early March. They remained in Geneva until May while Zinzendorf held discussions with the professors and pastors and translated Moravian works into French, as well as holding various services for his little "House Congregation." On May 16 they left Geneva for Basel, and then returned by water to Marienborn. As they left Geneva, they were stoned by a hostile group of people, which was Tannenberg's personal introduction to the persecution with which the Moravians had long been familiar.[7]

Although he resumed his studies at Marienborn and later at Herrnhut, Tannenberg finally decided to leave the Moravian schools and return to his parents, a decision he later attributed to "an inclination to the world and sin." His return in 1742 did not please his parents but he felt that he was "as free as a bird in the air" and old enough to do as he pleased. But, as he expressed it, the true Shepherd had not lost sight of his straying sheep and gave him no rest until after four years, on June 19, 1746, permission was granted for Tannenberg to return to Herrnhut. Apparently this was a family decision for it was about this time that his parents and brothers and sisters also moved to Herrnhut. In the days that followed, Tannenberg received what for the Moravians was the greatest pleasure in life, reception into the congregation and admittance to the Lord's Supper.

The next year was spent joyfully in Herrnhut, but then an unexpected call came to Tannenberg to join the Moravian community at Zeist, Holland (near Utrecht). Dutifully, Tannenberg set out for Zeist with Brother Jorde on September 23, 1748, arriving there on October 10. He discovered, however, that it was not the will of the "Little Lamb" (Jesus) that he remain there, but rather that he join a group of Brethren who were making preparations to leave for the new settlement of Bethlehem in Pennsylvania. By December 13 they were ready to leave Zeist, and they arrived in London on January 11, 1749.

It happened that Zinzendorf was also in London at that time and made it his special concern to make the group's stay in England enjoyable and edifying. He also spoke to the group and to each individual personally concerning his future life in America, and held a final communion service with them before their departure from London.[8]

By this time Tannenberg had developed a deep attachment to the Count, his "precious teacher." Later he was to write to Zinzendorf from America informing him of his religious condition and family life.[9] The highly sentimental language of the early Moravians was perhaps a convention—he addresses Zinzendorf as "tenderly beloved dear one," and "kisses him right heartily in the Spirit"—but it is clear that there is beneath the language a genuine respect and affection for the one who had formed his faith.

On February 20, the Sea Congregation began their twelve-week journey to America. The efficient Moravians left nothing to chance and, having planned for American settlements, had purchased a ship to provide passage. This group, called the John Nitschmarn Colony after its leading member, sailed on the *Irene,* a ship of eighty tons, with a crew of sixteen and mounted with two guns. On board, in addition to the colonists, were Christian David, the "godly carpenter" who had aroused Johann Tanneberger in Moravia, Matthew and Rosina Stach, pioneer missionaries to Greenland, and several of their Eskimo converts who had been on a visit to Europe. And flying above them all was the Moravian ensign, a lamb carrying a flag, set on a blood-colored field.[10]

The ship arrived in New York on May 12 and the colony then traveled overland to Bethlehem, arriving there on May 21. It had been planned that the many single people among the colonists should be married and on July 15, 1749, twenty-eight couples were married in what came to be remembered as "the Great Wedding." Among those married were David Tannenberg and Anna Rosina Kern.

Rosina Kern[11] had been born on March 2, 1723, in Ebersdorf near Löbau in Upper Lusatia (in which Berthelsdorf was also located). Her parents, Andreas Kern, a linen weaver, and Anna Helena (Pfeiffer), had also been a part of the religious awakening stemming from Herrnhut and her father had been imprisoned as a result. This in turn had aroused a religious concern in Rosina. Some time later, she visited Herrnhut and was convinced that "if there were God's children in the world, one would find them here." As a result she moved to Herrnhut during the same month that David Tannenberg came there. In 1748 she joined the group destined for Pennsylvania which was later joined by Tannenberg in Zeist.

One could imagine a romantic association between these two young people leading from Herrnhut to a marriage in Bethlehem, but the facts were probably less romantic, if no less interesting. Moravian marriages were arranged by the elders of the congregation. The town regulations of Lititz, Pennsylvania, for example, specified that "no marriages shall be contracted or made without the privity and approbation of the elders . . . nor shall anyone attempt to promote or make secret matches."[12] But even the approval of the elders was not final, for a proposed marriage, agreeable to the families involved and to the elders, was then submitted to the Savior for his approval. This was done by means of the lot. Slips of paper were made with the inscriptions "The Savior approves . . ." and "The Savior does not approve . . ." and the one drawn was taken to be the will of the Savior in the matter. While the method may no longer be appeal-

ing even to Moravians, it provided for a good number of success-
ful marriages. The elders of the closed Moravian communities,
after all, knew their families, the families apparently had some
choice in the selections, and the persons to be married, feeling
that the marriage had been arranged with the express approval
of their Savior, usually did their best to make a success of the
match. The sagacious Benjamin Franklin, on hearing of the
Moravian marriage customs, objected, "If the Matches are not
made by the mutual Choice of the Parties, some of them may
chance to be very unhappy. And so they may, answer'd my In-
former, if you let the Parties chuse for themselves. —Which
indeed I could not deny."[13]

Bethlehem was at this time the center of Moravian life in
America. An earlier attempt had been made to settle in Georgia
—John Wesley had sailed to Georgia on the same ship as the
first Moravian colonists and been deeply impressed by their faith
and devotion—but it had been abandoned because of the war between England and Spain. This group then accepted the offer
of the English evangelist George Whitefield to establish a settlement at Nazareth, Pennsylvania. Soon after that village was
begun, a larger settlement was planned eight miles south which
was named Bethlehem by Count Zinzendorf on Christmas Eve,
1741. A communal economic system (called the Economy) was
organized in Bethlehem, mainly under the capable direction of
Bishop August Gottlieb Spangenberg. Under this plan the
labor of all was placed at the disposal of the community. Various
industries were established and persons assigned to them by the
officials of the Economy. The purpose was not only to provide
for the needs of this frontier community, but equally important,
to support mission work among the Indians. The Moravians
were not visionaries, but practical men applying their business
knowledge to the end of giving God's message to the heathen,
and Bethlehem proved to be an economic as well as a religious
success over many years.

David Tannenberg came to Bethlehem as a joiner and presumably it was in this capacity that he entered the service of the
community, helping to erect the necessary buildings for this grow-

ing town. He must have shown, too, an aptitude for business, for on August 8, 1752, the family moved to Nazareth where he assumed the position of warden or business manager of the community.[14] His duties among the 143 inhabitants of Nazareth included such varied tasks as leading morning prayer, conducting business matters in Bethlehem, and assisting in the washing of the sheep. (On one occasion Tannenberg and several other Brethren tried taking the sheep through the creek as an alternative to washing them and found it a very satisfactory substitute.)

Nazareth was, however, a relatively remote and unprotected village and, the Indians having allied themselves with the French, the area was subject to Indian attack. For this reason Tannenberg moved his family back to the security of Bethlehem on December 11, 1754. Here they passed the next three years peacefully, again in the service of the community. It was during these years that their daughters were born: Anna Rosina on November 8, 1750, at Bethlehem; Maria Elisabeth at Nazareth on July 15, 1753; and Anna Maria at Nazareth on November 18, 1756.[15] They were, as Tannenberg expressed it, the gifts of the "Little Lamb."

2

Father Klemm

Tannenberg's career as an organ builder appears to have begun through an apprenticeship with an older Moravian organ builder, Johann Gottlob Klemm. After many years of estrangement from the Moravian Brethren, "Father" Klemm, as he was often called, joined the community at Bethlehem in November, 1757, and shortly thereafter took Tannenberg as his assistant in the repair of the Bethlehem organ and in the manufacture of two new organs at Nazareth. During the next four-and-a-half years the older craftsman passed on to Tannenberg the craft of organ building as he had learned it in Europe.

Klemm[16] had been born May 12, 1690, in a village near Dresden, where his father was employed as schoolmaster and organist. The father had hopes of his becoming a minister, and to this end Klemm studied in Freiberg and for two years at the University of Leipzig. However, he was disappointed in the university, where he had hoped to profit spiritually, and consequently lost all desire to study theology, although he did experience a kind of religious awakening there.

His disappointed father died soon thereafter and Klemm turned to the profession of organ building which he learned in Dresden. There is a tradition that Klemm learned the art from Andreas Silbermann—but more likely it was from his brother Gottfried, who lived in Dresden—and modern builders have noted parallel features in the Silbermann and Tannenberg organs which would suggest Klemm as the link between them.

In Dresden Klemm also became acquainted with Count Zinzendorf. The Count had rented the lower floor of Klemm's residence during a stay in the city and was holding services there. Klemm's wife began to attend the services and spoke to her husband of the beautiful addresses which the Count delivered. Klemm eventually became interested, too, and the two men were introduced. Their meeting took place in 1724. Later the Count invited Klemm and his wife to accompany him to Berthelsdorf so that Klemm could repair the organ there. In this way they became better acquainted and Zinzendorf suggested that the Klemms move to Herrnhut. They did not immediately decide to go, but in 1726 they did leave Dresden for Herrnhut. Thus it was that they were present on August 13, 1727, for the communion service in the Berthelsdorf church at which a great outpouring of God's Spirit was felt by all. The occasion was remembered as the birthday of the Renewed *Unitas Fratrum,* and is still celebrated as one of the most important festivals of the Moravian Church. Indeed, Klemm became one of the spiritual leaders at Herrnhut, conducting public services there, and serving as a teacher of boys.[17]

In the years that followed, as Herrnhut attracted more people of various religious persuasions, Klemm again became disillusioned with religion, fell out with Zinzendorf, and finally decided to leave for America. A group of Schwenkfelders, followers of Caspar Schwenkfeld von Ossig, the spiritualist reformer of Silesia, had taken refuge at Herrnhut and when a small company of them left for Pennsylvania, Klemm traveled with them. The trip lasted twenty-three weeks and one day, taking them through Pirna, Dresden, Wittenberg, Magdeburg, Hamburg, Altona, Amsterdam, Haarlem (where Klemm and his wife and children joined the main group), and Rotterdam. From there they took the ship *Pennsylvania Merchant* and arrived in Philadelphia on September 18, 1733.[18]

Klemm settled near Philadelphia, living as a Separatist, that is, having no religious fellowship, and worked there at his profession until 1745 or 1746. The most important organ he made during this period, for Trinity Episcopal Church in New York

City, was completed in 1741. Twenty-two years later, when the
church offered the organ for sale, an advertisement in the *New
York Gazette* described it as follows:

> To be sold by the Church Wardens, the organ in Trinity
> Church. The instrument is large, consisting of 26 stops, 10
> in the great organ, 10 in the choir organ, and 6 in the swell,
> 3 sets of keys, with a frontispiece of gilt pipes, and otherwise
> neatly adorned.[19]

The organ cost £520, New York currency, to which a £40 gratuity
was added.[20] Klemm's son, Johann, Jr. was appointed the organist for Trinity's new organ.[21]

It is also known that Klemm built an organ for Christ Lutheran Church, near Stouchsburg, Berks County, Pennsylvania, in
1752, at a cost of £127 3*s.* 4*d.* which was in use for eighty-five
years[22] and in that year or the next added a half register to the
organ in Trappe Lutheran Church, Montgomery County, Pennsylvania.[23] He also made at least one harpsichord, because the
Metropolitan Museum of Art in New York City now owns a
harpsichord with the inscription: *Johannes Clemm fecit Philadelphia 1739.*

But perhaps most interesting is the organ that Klemm installed in the Moravian Chapel at Bethlehem in 1746. The small
organ (*Orgel Positiv*) and "the organmaker Klemm" arrived in
Bethlehem on June 10 of that year and the organ was first played
by Brother John Pyrlaeus at a love feast on June 18. Klemm
took the occasion to renew old acquaintances and to inspect the
children's school at Nazareth before his return to Philadelphia.[24]

This was the organ that was in the Bethlehem Chapel during
Tannenberg's first years there. It was also the organ Benjamin
Franklin referred to in his autobiography when he wrote of his
visit to Bethlehem during the Indian unrest, "I was at their
church, where I was entertain'd with good musick, the organ
being accompanied with violins, hautboys, flutes, clarinets, etc."[25]

The Bethlehem organ invites mention of yet another Moravian organ builder known to Tannenberg. In 1751 Robert
Hartaffel,[26] an organ builder of Lancaster County, Pennsylvania,

visited Bethlehem to repair the organ. Born February 25, 1717, at Leidek in Bingenheim (Hessen-Darmstadt), he lived near Marienborn and made several clavichords for the Moravian "School of the Prophets" there and then came to America on the ship *Ann Galley* in 1746. He lived in or near Lititz for a time, where he and his wife were members of the Moravian Church, and then in Lancaster, where he died on November 7, 1782. Although he did some organ work in Lancaster, Hartaffel apparently gave up his organ building for the tobacco business and, with his son-in-law, Christopher Demuth, began a tobacco business in Lancaster in 1770 which is still prospering there as Demuths Tobacco Shop.

Perhaps the visit of Hartaffel to Bethlehem, or merely the presence of Klemm's organ there, had already aroused Tannenberg's interest in organ building by the time that Klemm returned to Bethlehem to spend his last days there. In 1745 or 1746 Klemm's wife had died and he had moved to New York City where he had renewed his associations with the Moravians. A visitor from Bethlehem told him of the need for a new organ in Nazareth and Klemm wrote to Bishop Spangenberg, asking permission to spend his last days in Bethlehem and offering his services as an organ builder. Permission was granted and Klemm arrived in Bethlehem on November 25, 1757. He was soon put to work repairing the Bethlehem organ.

The first reference to Tannenberg's association with Klemm appears in the Bethlehem diary for January 15 of the following year when Tannenberg traveled to Philadelphia to buy boards for an organ. Then on March 1, 1758, Klemm, Tannenberg, and Tannenberg's family left Bethlehem for Nazareth to take up residence in Nazareth Hall and begin the construction of two organs, which were completed by the end of the year.[27] On January 29, 1759, Klemm and Tannenberg also installed a new organ in the Bethlehem Chapel, replacing the 1746 organ, which was moved temporarily to Nazareth. Later that year, Klemm and the Tannenbergs moved from Nazareth Hall to the "Nursery," the residence of the Economy of Nazareth and Bethlehem for children whose parents were missionaries or otherwise engaged in the

work of the Economy. The Nursery was located in what is now
known as Whitefield House. Both Nazareth Hall and Whitefield House, impressive stone buildings, are still standing in Nazareth and suggest a prosperity and elegance which one would not
ordinarily expect of a frontier village in the 1750s.

During this period the two builders also made an organ for
the Moravian settlement at Christian's Spring, near Nazareth,
and the consecration services for the new organ in 1760 give a
glimpse into Moravian life in that early, semirural setting. Bishop
Spangenberg and other prominent citizens of Bethlehem arrived
at noon on July 10 to consecrate the new chapel and organ. Following this service, they proceeded to the fields where a love feast
(a fellowship meal, usually of buns and coffee) was held for the
reapers. The musicians accompanied the group and during the
love feast an ode, written for the occasion by Brother Tannenberg, was sung solo. Brother Graff recited a poem dedicated to
the workers of the fields, and the boys, led by Brother Albrecht,
performed on their musical instruments. In the evening, the first
song service was held in the new chapel with its new organ.[28]

Several weeks after this occasion, on August 8, 1760, Klemm
and the Tannenbergs left Nazareth to take up residence in the
house of a deceased Moravian, James Burnside, up the Monocacy
Creek from Bethlehem. Here, somewhat isolated from the Moravian community, they set up their organ shop and completed at
least one more organ, for Bethabara, North Carolina. Here, old
Father Klemm passed his last days, regretting—according to the
church officials—his disagreements with Zinzendorf, and weeping
at past errors and present joys. And here he died on May 5,
1762.

Klemm's death left Tannenberg's profession in question.
The elders at one point expressed the opinion that he should give
up organ building, which "is tied up with a good deal of disorder,"
move back to Bethlehem, and devote himself to cabinetmaking.[29]
Perhaps their real objection was a fear that organ building might
lead to too much contact with the outside world, especially in view
of Klemm's history of Separatism. But although Tannenberg
was a loyal member of the community—he and his wife served

during this time as *Jünger*, disciples or leaders of the married couples in Bethlehem[30]—he was always a somewhat independent spirit. He chose to continue as an organ builder, and apparently convinced the reluctant elders.

Another obstacle appeared in the form of John Antes, a young man who was later to establish himself as an outstanding musician, composer, and missionary to Egypt. Tannenberg complained to the elders that Antes was beginning to make harpsichords and similar instruments, and that this was damaging his business. Tannenberg now had a wife and four children to support (a son, Johann David, had been born on September 13, 1760) and there was only a limited demand for keyboard instruments. He had, however, no objection to Antes' continuing to make stringed instruments and the elders agreed that Antes should confine himself to these in the future.[31]

There was also an encouraging development. In 1764, Georg Andreas Sorge, Court and City Organist at Lobenstein, Germany, sent to his "friends in Pennsylvania" a manuscript entitled "The Secret Art of the Measurement of Organ Pipes." It was a theoretical work, setting forth the mathematical basis for the construction of organ pipes, an essential tool for the skilled organ builder. Two copies of the manuscript are now in Moravian repositories and it is almost certain that the work was used by Tannenberg.[32] When the 1798 Tannenberg organ in Winston-Salem was being restored, the old pipes were checked against the drawings in Sorge's treatise and it was clear that Tannenberg had used the same measurements in making his pipes.[33] With this new theoretical understanding of his craft to add to the experience gained by working with Klemm, Tannenberg was now ready to launch his new career in a new home, the Moravian community of Lititz in Lancaster County, Pennsylvania.

3

Lititz

*It's a kindly, softly, country there, back of Philadelphia
among the German towns, Lancaster way. Little houses and
bursting big barns, fat cattle, fat women, and all as peaceful
as Heaven might be if they farmed there.*

—*Rudyard Kipling*[34]

The land that appealed to Kipling has appealed to many
others as well. General John Sutter, on whose California
land gold was discovered in 1848, passed through the village of
Lititz in Lancaster County in 1871 and decided to make it his
home. When he died, although he was not a Moravian, he was
permitted burial in the cemetery of the Brethren, where he lies
now, one of Count Zinzendorf's more unlikely heirs.[35]

It may have been the same features which impressed Kipling
and Sutter that drew David Tannenberg to Lititz in Lancaster
County, or it may only have been the desire to find a location
better suited to his profession. In either case the area was not
entirely new to him. In November, 1761, he had gone to Lititz,
taking with him the old Klemm organ that had been in the Bethlehem Chapel and had now been sold to the Lititz congregation for
£40. He stayed there nine days, installing the organ in the Single
Sisters' House, which was then serving also as the congregational
meeting place, and paying a brief visit to Lancaster.[36] Again in
April, 1765, Tannenberg went by way of Lititz to Lancaster to
install a new organ, ordered two-and-a-half years before, in the
Moravian Chapel. He stayed in Lancaster from April 20 to May

18

6 setting up the organ and also repairing a house organ belonging to George Ross, who was later to become one of the signers of the Declaration of Independence. Mrs. Ross took the occasion to examine and play Tannenberg's new organ in the Moravian Chapel.[37]

Preparations were made that same year to move to Lititz and on August 16, 1765, Tannenberg, his wife and two of their children, Rosina and David, arrived in Lititz rejoicing that, after the isolation of the Burnside House, they were again to be living within a Moravian community. They purchased what was called the *Pilgerhaus*, a two-story stone house, thirty by forty feet, located at the center of the town. The house had been built by George Klein, the founder of Lititz, in 1754. It was, in fact, the first house in Lititz and had been used at first as the meeting place of the congregation and then as a tavern and store. The house has since been torn down but one wall was retained and can be seen at the rear of the present structure. Some time later a small, stone shop was built at the rear of the house; here the organs were built. An old log stable completed the buildings on the property.[38]

"Liesel" (Maria Elisabeth) and Anna Maria had been left temporarily in Bethlehem when the family moved. After the birth of their fifth and last child, Samuel, on April 23, 1766, Tannenberg wrote to the church officials in Bethlehem asking that Liesel be sent to help with the increased housework.[39] She arrived in Lititz in July, 1766. Her sister, Anna Maria, came the following October.

The town of Lititz, in which the entire family was now settled, had been founded in Warwick Township, about seven miles from Lancaster, on a farm donated to the Moravians by George Klein. At Zinzendorf's suggestion it was called Lititz after the place in Bohemia where the *Unitas Fratrum* was first organized. This was to be exclusively a Moravian community and permanent residence was granted only to members of the church. In spiritual affairs the town was governed by the Elders' Conference and the minister, in temporal affairs by the warden and the *Aufseher Collegium* (Committee of Oversight), which was elected by the Church Council. Private residences were permitted, but there were also communal residences known as the Single Sisters' House and the Single Brethren's House, where these little congregations or "choirs" lived and worked under the direction of a chaplain and a warden. The other choirs which were similarly organized but without common residences were the married couples, the widows, the widowers, the little boys, little girls, and infants. Each choir had its own hymns and liturgies, rules, meetings, and anniversaries, and shared in love feasts and worship services. The choirs to which the females belonged could be recognized by the color of the ribbon with which their white linen caps were tied: red for the children; light red for the older girls; pink for the single sisters; blue for the married women; and white for widows.

When Tannenberg settled in Lititz, he was required to sign the forty-five "Town Regulations"[40] which would govern his and his family's life in both spiritual and temporal affairs as long as they lived there. The regulations vividly depict life in Lititz.

> That no Inhabitant follow any other Trade or Business, save that only which he followed at his Admission into the Village, unless he obtain the Consent and Approbation of the Committee for so doing.
>
> That no one give even a Night's Lodging, in his House, to any Person whatsoever, without having first acquainted the Committee thereof and obtained their or the Warden's Approbation. In like manner, that no Inhabitant nor any belonging to him, by his Direction, undertake a Journey, either far or near without consulting the Warden thereupon.
>
> Nothing shall be taught or preached in Lititz, but what is conformable to the Gospel of Christ. Has an one an Opinion, peculiar to himself, such a Person may be indulged provided he seek not to propogate it.
>
> No meetings without Light, shall be suffered on any Account whatsoever.
>
> No Dancing Matches, Taverning (except for the necessary Entertainment of Strangers and Travellers), Beer-Tappings, Feastings at Weddings, Christenings or Burials, Common Sports and Pastimes, nor the playing of the Chil-

dren in the Streets, shall be so much as heard of amongst the Inhabitants. They that have Inclinations that Way bent cannot live at Lititz.

Should any person by the all-wise Providence of God be deprived of his Senses, he shall for God's Sake be mercifully treated and patiently borne with . . . . And if so be he is restored again no Mention shall be made of his former Situation in any wise.

It is quite necessary that every One make his Last Will in due Season.

The town regulations were strictly enforced and the minutes of the Elders' Conference and the Committee of Oversight include frequent discussions of infractions of each of them. Tannenberg, too, was often the subject of discussion. Shortly after he had moved to Lititz, he apparently began to raise fruit, a common venture among the Pennsylvania Germans. Immediately the matter was brought up: "Tannenberg is beginning to devote himself to fruit-raising. We do not like this. We fear that it will be a danger to his profession and his children."[41] On another occasion, he had asked the tailor to make him a pair of red trousers and the project was immediately denounced by the elders as an act that would lead the young people into "clothing foolishness." Brother Grube was to ask him to change the order and, if he would not, the master tailor was to be asked not to fill it.[42] Again, the single sisters were forbidden to attend funerals in the country and when Tannenberg took his daughter Rosina to such a funeral he was sharply reprimanded and Rosina was punished.[43]

These restrictions must have caused some dissatisfaction, yet it must also be said that, at least among the older generation, the regulations had been freely accepted and were in general gladly obeyed. There was a tone of joy and contentment in the community, born of the knowledge that it was being led by the servants of him "in whose service is perfect freedom." One visitor to Bethlehem—not a Moravian himself—wrote with a certain wistfulness of the life he had tasted there.

> Setting aside their ridiculous mode of entering into the marriage state, and which to them is of little moment, I could not but reflect, if content was in this life they enjoy it. Far from the bustle of a troublesome world, living in perfect liberty, each one pursuing his own ideas and inclinations, and residing in the most healthful situation imaginable, which is so healthy, that they are subject to few, if any diseases.
>
> As want is a stranger, so is vice. Their total ignorance of the refined elegancies of life, precludes any anxiety or regret that they possess not wealth to enjoy them. Nevertheless, they possess what many are entire strangers to, who are surrounded with what are termed blessings, those true and essential ones—health and tranquillity of mind.[44]

However, it is also true that among the younger generation, especially after the Revolution, which brought the outside world into the heart of Lititz, there appeared a growing dissatisfaction with the old ways, a dissatisfaction which was to raise many difficulties in the Tannenberg home.

Life in a Moravian community also offered certain benefits and one of the most important for Tannenberg must have been the musical life of the community. When Tannenberg arrived in Lititz, the community boasted, in addition to an organ, at least two violins, one bass, and two French horns.[45] From an early date there was also a trombone quartet in Lititz as in most of the Moravian communities. Descendants of the German *Stadtpfeifer,* who serenaded Germany from the church towers and castle ramparts, the Moravian trombonists were used to announce public events such as weddings, funerals, and church festivals. They were especially noted for their predawn announcement of the arrival of Easter, announcing with their chorales that the people were to arise and gather in the church, and later leading them from there to the cemetery—God's Acre—where the concluding services were held.[46]

Lititz, like Bethlehem, also had a kind of community orchestra called the *collegium musicum,* such a group having been organized among the men of Lititz in the year 1765 by the Rev. Bernhard Adam Grube.[47] Tannenberg was not only an organist, but also a violinist (or perhaps a violist) and as such took part in the activities of the orchestra. Another member of the orchestra was the violinist Tobias Hirte. Hirte was the town character— a schoolteacher, author, and itinerant peddler of "Seneca Oil," petroleum which he gathered from pools north of Fort Pitt and sold for medicinal purposes. Rudyard Kipling somehow learned of Hirte and used him in two of his stories, describing him as "the famous Seneca Oil man, that lived half of every year among the Indians," selling medicine out of saddlebags and sleeping in friends' farmhouses.[48]

The orchestra was called on to perform for visitors, as when the Attorney General of the United States, Edmund Randolph, stopped in Lititz in 1791. Randolph, a former Governor of Virginia, expressed a desire to hear the orchestra and Brother Müller, the leader, was hurriedly recalled from a visit to Lancaster to assemble the orchestra and present a concert.[49] Lest it be thought that the cultured Attorney General might have been amused at an amateur performance, it should be noted that the library of the orchestra contained chamber works of some fifty European composers, including Boccherini, Handel, Haydn, and Mozart.[50] (Some of these works, like Haydn's *Creation,* received their first American performances by Moravian groups.) Johannes Herbst, the pastor of the Lititz Church from 1791 to 1811 and a prolific composer and copyist, added his own collection of nearly one thousand handwritten scores to the Lititz library. These scores indicate that the *collegium musicum* at that time was composed of at least a string quartet, if not a double quartet, plus two horns, and two flutes. It is the judgment of one student of these scores that, "the difficulty of some of the parts, and the rapidity with which new works were studied, indicates that Herbst's performers were fairly capable."[51]

Herbst was among a group of Moravian composers who have only recently been recognized as the first real composers to work in America. During this "unknown century of American music" a wealth of compositions was produced, equal in quality to those produced in Europe at the same time. In addition to Herbst several other Moravian composers either worked or visited in Lititz, notably Johann Friedrich Peter, Jeremiah Dencke, George Godfrey Müller, and Christian Gregor.

Tannenberg contributed to the musical life of Lititz also as a vocalist. He and Brother Andreas Albrecht, the village gunsmith, were the church's *cantores* and, as such, sang at least for the church's festive occasions. One of several of these occasions recorded was in 1771. Brother Gregor had prepared a psalm for the annual festival of the Single Brethren's Choir. It was distributed to those present, and then Albrecht and Tannenberg sang it while Brother Grube accompanied them at the organ.[52]

But Tannenberg's participation in the life of the community was not limited to its music. He was also a participant and leader in both the religious and secular life of the village. In 1768 he was admitted as an acolyte—presumably an assistant in the worship services. He was frequently chosen as one of the foot washers during Holy Week services, and also participated in the "Hourly Intercession," the round-the-clock prayer groups which were organized on behalf of Moravian missions.

More important was his contribution to the secular affairs of Lititz. Tannenberg held many offices in the village over the years, most of them having to do with business and financial affairs. He is mentioned as collector or treasurer for various funds, and also served a term as township assessor. He served for many years on the Church Council, the Committee of Oversight, and at times on the Helpers' Conference and the Greater Helpers' Conference, the latter two being advisory groups to the central management of the Moravian communities. As a member of the Committee of Oversight he often served the community as executor or guardian in the affairs of deceased villagers. In the same way he was often delegated to speak to people on behalf of the committee, for example to two parties who were fighting over an apple tree which was on their property line,[53] or to one of the Brethren who should be discouraged from helping his son to sell his house.[54] These are responsibilities that would be given to a man of good judgment and some tact, who had not only the necessary business experience, but also the respect of his neighbors. These qualities would be necessary, too, in the *Fremden-*

diener, or servant of the visitors, an office which Tannenberg was called on to fill. The character of the man becomes clearer as he is seen speaking with his neighbors about their apple tree, arranging the affairs of a young ward, or taking time out from his organ work in Philadelphia to write to the Brethren about a man who has a claim on some property in Lititz which Tannenberg hopes to settle.[55] In these various ways Tannenberg served the Lititz Brethren while he established his reputation as a master organ builder in Pennsylvania and the surrounding states.

4

The Roll of Fame

After his move to Lititz, Tannenberg devoted himself fully to organ building and, during his thirty-nine years there, produced an average of an organ each year. Although the organs were built in his shop at Lititz, their installation and tuning and the tuning and repair of other organs meant that Tannenberg traveled extensively, often spending weeks or months outside the community of the Brethren. These travels were mainly in Pennsylvania, but they took him also into New York, New Jersey, and Maryland.

Most of this travel and organ work was done among German-speaking people. The Germans had settled widely, not only in Pennsylvania, but also in Maryland and down the Shenandoah Valley into Virginia and North Carolina. In 1766, Benjamin Franklin reported to a committee of the House of Commons that the Germans were estimated to compose a third of Pennsylvania's population.[56] In large areas of eastern Pennsylvania, German was almost exclusively the language that was spoken and in both Pennsylvania and Maryland provision had been made for printing state laws in German as well as English. In 1795 the Congress of the United States failed by only one vote to take the same action.[57] Almost all of the Moravian records of this period are in German as are the records of the churches for which Tannenberg built organs. There is, indeed, no evidence that Tannenberg spoke English, although one would assume that, like the widely traveled Moravian ministers, he could use the language

26

if it were necessary. But it was primarily for the Germans that Tannenberg built his organs.

The Moravian officials were greatly concerned, especially in the earlier years, with the travels of their members. They recorded their departures, arrivals, and destinations meticulously in the diaries, both as a matter of interest to the other Moravian communities who would read them and, one suspects, as a form of social control over the members. As a result, Tannenberg's travels can be closely followed in the diaries of the various Moravian communities.

In October, 1766, Tannenberg spent a week in Philadelphia setting up an organ for an unnamed citizen of that city.[58] The next fall he took an organ to Albany, New York, traveling by way of Brunswick and New York City. On his return trip he repaired the organ in the Moravian Church in New York City and delivered letters and reports of that church to the officials in Philadelphia. In all, he was gone from Lititz seven-and-a-half weeks.[59] In 1768 he spent a few days in Philadelphia on business and later installed a new organ at Maxatawny, Berks County, Pennsylvania.[60] In June, 1769, he repaired two organs in Reading, Pennsylvania, and in September and October was away for six weeks, installing an organ at the New Goshenhoppen Church in Montgomery County, Pennsylvania, and repairing the two organs in the Moravian Church in Philadelphia.[61] In 1770 he repaired an organ in Frederick, Maryland, and set up new organs in Moselem and Lancaster in Pennsylvania.

Tannenberg's organs were of great interest to his neighbors, and with each new work his fame grew. When the organ for Albany was finished, Tannenberg set it up in Lititz and a crowd of people, mostly from Philadelphia, but also from Lancaster and other places, and including a party of Quakers, came to see and hear it.[62] Again the following year, when the Maxatawny organ was completed "many music lovers" from Lancaster—a Lutheran and a Reformed preacher among them—came to Lititz to hear it.[63]

It was, however, the consecration of Tannenberg's fifteen-stop organ in the German Reformed Church in Lancaster that

securely established his reputation. The Philadelphia newspapers
carried glowing reports of the organ and its maker. The corre-
spondent of the *Pennsylvania Gazette* wrote this account:

> Lancaster, Pennsylvania, December 24, 1770. Yester-
> day we had the pleasure of hearing for the first time the new
> organ of the High Dutch Reformed Church, of this place,
> accompanied with a variety of vocal music composed for the
> occasion, which I may venture to say, not only proved by my
> own experience, but the approbation of all present, was never
> equalled in any place of worship in the province or perhaps
> on the continent. The organ was made by David Tanne-
> berger of Lititz—a Moravian town nearby—and I dare ven-
> ture to assert, is much superior in workmanship and sweet-
> ness of sound to any made by the late celebrated Mr.
> Feyering, who was so generally taken notice of for his in-
> genuity. It does great honor to the maker and is worth the
> attention and notice of the curious who may happen to pass
> this way. It will doubtless recommend him to all who are
> desirous of having work of that nature.[64]

The comparison with Feyring was significant. Previously the
accolades for organ building in Philadelphia—which was *the*
center of culture—had been given not to any of the Moravian
builders but to Philip Feyring (or Feuering), a German Lutheran
who had died of consumption in 1767 at the age of thirty-seven.
Feyring had been born September 5, 1730, at Arfeld, Germany,[65]
and had come to America in his youth where he soon gained a
reputation as a maker of musical instruments, especially of spinets
and harpsichords.[66] His work was known to such men as "Baron"
Henry William Stiegel, the iron- and glass-maker, and Henry
Melchior Muhlenberg, the patriarch of the Lutheran Church
in America.[67]

Feyring also gained fame as an organ builder. As early as
1755, when he was only twenty-four years old, he contracted with
the German Reformed Church in Philadelphia to reconstruct an
organ which the officers had bought elsewhere, and again in
1767 he worked on this organ. In 1763 he was paid for work
on the organ in the Market Square Church in Germantown.[68]

His major accomplishment was the construction of new organs for the three Episcopal churches in Philadelphia—one for St. Paul's in 1762, one for St. Peter's in 1764, and one for Christ Church in 1766.[69] The cases of Feyring's works can still be seen in St. Peter's and Christ Churches.

When the organ for St. Paul's had been completed, a long poem appeared in the *Gazette* entitled "On Hearing the Organ at St. Paul's Church, on Christmas Day, 1762," which concluded with this lavish praise:

> Whilst Organ's dulcet Notes the Breast inspire
> With true devotion, and a sacred Fire;
> Thy name, O Fyring thy deserving Name
> Shall shine conspicuous in the Roll of Fame;
> Ages to come, and Men in future Days
> Shall greateful pay their Tribute to thy Praise.[70]

Yet only eight years later Tannenberg's name had replaced Feyring's on the "roll of fame" and today the name of Feyring is all but forgotten.

As Tannenberg's reputation grew, so did the volume of work. By the fall of 1770 the elders had discussed the situation, concluding that since people had to wait so long for their organs, Tannenberg should have more help.[71] The next few years were indeed busy ones. Organs were built for and installed in churches in Reading, Lebanon, Lancaster, and Easton in Pennsylvania, and in Frederick, Maryland. In 1771 Tannenberg spent over two months in Philadelphia tuning and repairing organs.[72] In 1775 he went to Bethlehem to repair the organ there,[73] and in 1777 to Reading to tune and repair his organ in the Lutheran Church.[74]

One of the organs from this period, the one built for Trinity Lutheran Church in Lancaster in 1774, was an especially fine instrument. A unique contemporary description of it indicates the kind of impression that Tannenberg's work was making. The description was written by Thomas Anburey, a lieutenant in the British Army of General Burgoyne. He was captured at the Battle of Saratoga and taken as a prisoner to Charlottesville,

Virginia, by way of Pennsylvania. In December of 1778 he was
in Lancaster where he visited the Lutheran Church with its four-
year-old Tannenberg organ. He gave this description of the
church and its organ in a letter dated December 17, 1778.

> The town of Lancaster has no building of any conse-
> quence, except the Lutheran Church, which is only built of
> brick, the inside has a most magnificent appearance; the large
> galleries on each side, the spacious organ loft, supported by
> Corinthian pillars, are exceedingly beautiful, and there are
> pillars of the Ionic order, from the galleries to the roof. The
> altar-piece is very elegantly ornamented; the whole of the
> church, as well as the organ, painted white with gilt decora-
> tions, which has a very neat appearance; it greatly reminded
> me of the chapel at Greenwich Hospital; the organ is reck-
> oned the largest and best in America, it was built by a Ger-
> man, who resides about 17 miles from Lancaster, he made
> every individual part of it with his own hands; it was near
> 7 years in compleating; the organ has not only every pipe and
> stop that is in most others, but it has many other pipes to swell
> the bass, which are of an amazing circumference, and these
> are played upon by the feet, there being a row of wooden
> keys that the performer treads on. I do not recollect ever
> seeing an organ of this construction, except those of the Savoy
> Chapel and St. Paul's; in the latter they are shut up as the
> vibration of sound was found too powerful for the dome;
> but then they had only 4 or 5 of these wooden keys, whereas
> this organ has a dozen: the man who shewed the instrument
> played on it, and the effect of these keys was astonishing, it
> absolutely made the very building shake. It is the largest,
> and I think the finest I ever saw, without exception; and
> when you examine it, you wonder it did not take up the
> man's whole life in constructing; to estimate its goodness and
> value, I shall only tell you it cost two thousand five hundred
> pounds sterling; to you who are so musical, what a treat
> would it be to be here a few hours only, unless indeed, you
> would think a few more not thrown away entirely, when
> allotted to
>
> Yours, etc.[75]

There is considerable exaggeration in Anburey's letter; Lititz is only seven miles from Lancaster; Tannenberg certainly made most of the organ himself, but others are known to have helped, for example in the carpentry work on the case; it could not have taken seven years to make the organ, since the decision to purchase an organ was not made until 1771; and the price is highly inflated—the actual price is not known, but it must have been nearer four- to five-hundred pounds. Nevertheless, the exaggerations themselves convey something of the awe which the organ created in its listeners. And this much was true; there were no other organs to compare with Tannenberg's in the whole of America.

But fame and reputation were soon followed by dishonor in the Tannenberg family. Tannenberg himself may have considered it as God's way of humbling him, for he had written in his memoir that God had taught him in a blessed way in life, seeking always to bring him closer to the mind of God. One of the things he may have learned is that humility comes sometimes only through humiliation.

On August 5, 1776, there were no evening prayers in the Single Sisters' House. Instead the Sisters were gathered together and addressed by Sister Maria Magdalena who informed them with a sad heart that Rosina Tannenberg and Gertraut Baumgartner had been seduced into unchastity by Samuel Fockel, one of the married men, thus bringing shame on the entire choir and pain to the dear Savior. The event was presented to them as a warning and the married Brethren were also informed that they must be on their guard, faithfully watching over their children day and night.

Rosina, however, was no child—she was then twenty-five years old—and the exact circumstances of the situation are not clear. It is clear that Samuel Fockel was judged to be guilty of adultery and was given notice that he must leave the village within four weeks. Gertraut Baumgartner is referred to as being a deceiver as well as being herself deceived and was also expelled from the community. Rosina Tannenberg was thought to have played a less guilty part in the affair and was allowed to remain

in Lititz, but no longer as a member of the choir or as a participant in the Lord's Supper.

Gertraut Baumgartner's oft-repeated entreaties to reenter
the community were denied, but there was mercy for Rosina.
After fifteen months she was readmitted to the Single Sisters'
Choir and to the communion. After dinner on November 15,
1777, the Sisters were informed by Sister Maria Magdalena of
the elders' decision of readmittance. At seven o'clock the Sisters
gathered and took Rosina into their midst while Bishop Hehl
addressed them. Then Rosina knelt and received absolution from
Sister Maria Magdalena with the laying on of hands.[76] Thus
the rift between Rosina and the community was overcome just at
the time that the community itself was to be torn apart by the
American Revolution.

5

The War of the Revolution

The revolution against England was a matter of concern to the Moravian Brethren from its beginning. In 1775 the diarist at Lititz recorded a brief footnote to history: "Congress having adopted a measure regarding the use of tea, which is now strictly obeyed everywhere, it was resolved to sell none of it in our store," and followed it with the news of "the bloody action" at Bunker Hill and Charlestown.[77]

Bethlehem, because of its large buildings and its crucial position on one of the main roads between New England and the Middle Colonies, soon saw national events at first hand as high officers and government officials began to pass through the town. Most of the important names of the Revolution appear in the Bethlehem diary and the Brethren noted with some pride the satisfaction which visitors expressed on seeing the town. No small part of their satisfaction was in seeing and hearing the musical riches of the community, and especially the organs, as these extracts from the Bethlehem diary demonstrate:

December 17, 1776. Generals Gates, Sullivan, Arnold, Stirling, Glover, and about thirty officers, at dusk came to attend our meeting, but owing to confusion in the town it was dropped. They were taken into the chapel to hear the organ, and were pleased with the music.

September 22, 1777. Sixteen Congressmen at Bethlehem (John Hancock, John Adams, Richard Henry Lee, Henry Laurens, William Duer and others) were escorted through

the Sisters' House where they were entertained with singing
and playing on the organ.

June 15, 1779. Early this morning Lady Washington
arrived from Easton, in company with Generals Sullivan,
Poor, and Maxwell, and some twenty officers—in the evening
with her escort attended the service and listened to the organ
played.

July 25, 1782. General Washington, two aides and
escort arrived. They visited the chapel, where they were entertained with cake and wine, while Rev. Jacob Van Vleck
played on the organ. They also attended the service, after
which the church choir entertained their guests with sacred
music, both vocal and instrumental.[78]

War, of course, meant more than cakes and wine with organ
music; it meant soldiers and bloodshed as well. The Moravians
tried valiantly to avoid any association with this aspect of the
war, and the church members were counseled to be loyal to the
oath they had taken to the king and to refrain from bearing
arms. Their position was primarily not political but religious;
they were honoring those who ruled and were refraining from
murder. On the other hand, they were willing to pay war taxes
and when "non-associators," that is, those who could not con-
scientiously bear arms, were assessed in Lancaster County, David
Tannenberg was appointed collector by the Brethren in Lititz,
the diarist noting that "the contribution in money we regard as
purely a township affair."[79]

A more difficult situation was presented to the Brethren
when they received notice to appear for military drill. At first
conscientious objectors were excused on the payment of a fine,
but even then many of the younger Brethren had to be persuaded
that the aversion of the elders to drilling was more important
than the three-pound, ten-shilling fine.[80] By 1777 the situation
had grown worse and all men between the ages of eighteen and
fifty-three were to be enrolled in the militia. The Brethren in
Lititz responded by boycotting the muster. The Lieutenant of
Militia then came to Lititz to announce that each man must
either appear or provide a substitute, but the Brethren would do

neither, and when soldiers appeared to take them away the young men ran and hid themselves in the woods. Matters continued in this uncertain way for several weeks until October 21, 1777, when six armed militiamen entered the chapel of the Single Brethren's House in Lititz, read out the names of nine single men who had been called to the militia and, when they responded, put them under guard. Five married men were also taken, among them the forty-nine-year-old David Tannenberg. They were marched to Manheim (five miles away) and kept under guard for the night.

> The next day they were taken to Lancaster and, to the accompaniment of drum and fife, through a dense mass of people, with cries of "Tories" from every side, were marched to the Quaker meeting house, where they were locked up with many others who, like themselves, had been thus forcibly dragged together. Here their room was so limited that they could neither sit nor lie down; and besides, they had very little to eat. The brethren and sisters of Lancaster, however, did all they could for their comfort, particularly Brother Hobson, through whose influence they were released from their prison and quartered, for the night, among our church members. Neither must they return to confinement, but could go about the city freely, Brother Hobson having given his word for them.[81]

The Brethren had influential friends in Lancaster, including Brother William Henry, wealthy gunsmith, steamboat pioneer, and Revolutionary patriot, and through their intercession the arrests were declared illegal and the men were allowed to return to Lititz the next day. It was the kind of incident that the Moravians had learned to expect in their history and the diarist's reflection on it has a tone of calm resignation:

> It seems, then, that we, too, must suffer. For help we can depend only upon our dear Father in Heaven, who, in this dreadful time of war and confusion, must shield and guide us; for surely, He knows that we are his Son's people, and have nothing to do with the world and its quarrels.[82]

This affair had hardly been settled when it was announced
that General Washington had chosen Lititz as the site for a
military hospital and that 250 sick and wounded soldiers were
to be quartered there.[83] While Lititz was not immediately acces-
sible to the battlefields, it had the advantage of large, stone
buildings, quite suitable for hospital use. The year before, the
Single Brethren's House in Bethlehem had been taken over for
hospital use and it was the Single Brethren's House in Lititz
which was also chosen. The entire community was dismayed—
they realized that the arrival of hundreds of soldiers would
profoundly disturb the life of the village—but Tannenberg must
have been especially dismayed. On November 30, 1776, he had
installed a new organ in the Single Brethren's House in Bethlehem only to have that building occupied by the military one
week later. And now the soldiers were invading the Lititz
Single Brethren's House where he had also installed a new organ
just four months before.

On December 19, 1777, eighty sick soldiers arrived. The
next day fifteen wagons filled with soldiers came, and the following day one hundred more soldiers, who had to be sent elsewhere for lack of space. The religious community's attitude was
one of self-concern rather than of compassion. They wanted
nothing to do with the world and its quarrels or its wounded;
but the misery of the scene began slowly to change their attitude.
The doctors themselves became sick and the soldiers lay unat-
tended. A snowstorm kept the nearly recovered inside among
those sick with "camp fever." On December 31 another wagon-
load of sick soldiers arrived and by January 1, there were seven
dead. Still, as the Brethren's sympathy grew, so did their annoy-
ances. Some of the little boys began to trade with the soldiers,
receiving cartridges and powder which they set off in the barns,
and Tobias Hirte acquired a gun which he was promptly ordered
to dispose of. A "bad, independent World Spirit" had been let
loose in the village and the elders feared for the souls of the
young people.

Early in the new year, Dr. William Brown, Physician General of the Middle Department of the Continental Army, was

transferred to Lititz and placed in charge of all the surrounding military hospitals. By this time space in the village was at a premium and the army officers were lodged in private homes. Dr. Brown was quartered with the Tannenbergs.[84] This circumstance meant that Tannenberg would have the opportunity of being well informed about national affairs. Dr. Brown was a man of culture, had his degree from the University of Edinburgh, and was well acquainted with the leaders of the Revolution, especially Washington, Jefferson, and Madison.[85] Brown's relations with his host and the other Brethren during his seven-month stay must have been amicable, for in 1779 he returned with his family for a visit. "He was very friendly and declares himself delighted to meet the Brethren again. He wished we had a settlement in Virginia."[86]

While living with the Tannenbergs, Dr. Brown prepared a thirty-two page book in Latin which is regarded as the first pharmacopoeia published in the United States. The preface of this little book, dated March 12, 1778, at Lititz, describes it as a

> repertory of simple and efficacious prescriptions for the use of the military hospital belonging to the army . . . adapted especially to our present state of need and poverty, which we owe to the ferocious cruelty of the enemy, and to a cruel war brought unexpectedly upon our fatherland.[87]

In April it was rumored that Lititz was to be entirely vacated to make room for the army's general hospital. Bishop Hehl dispatched a plaintive letter to Dr. William Shippen ("Do not draw down upon you the tears and sighings of so many helpless ones . . .") whose reply revealed that this action was now thought not to be necessary.[88] Finally, in August, 1778, after nine months of occupation, the remaining soldiers were moved to other hospitals and the Single Brethren's House was returned to the community. During this time more than five hundred, probably nearer a thousand, soldiers had been quartered there. A hundred and twenty of the soldiers had died at the hospital, most of whom were buried shoulder-to-shoulder in trenches south of the town. Nine

Moravians also died during this period, at least four of them of "camp fever."

Even before the evacuation of the hospital, the town was afflicted in a new way. In 1777 a Test Act had been passed which required of all citizens an oath of allegiance to the new government and an abjuration of the king. The official position of the Moravians was that the test should not be taken and a petition was presented to the Congress asking that Moravians be exempted from its requirements. In the meantime, the church ruled that anyone who took the oath required by the Test Act would be excluded from the communion.[89]

On May 31, 1778, the members of the Lititz congregation learned that twenty-two of their members—"who gradually had been revealing themselves"—had gone to Lancaster and taken the oath of allegiance, forswearing the king. At the head of the list stood the name of David Tannenberg. Unfortunately, the motivation of the group is not known. Tannenberg, unless he had changed his opinions since his imprisonment, was by no means an ardent patriot. It seems more likely that he and the group felt some sympathy for the new government and, in any case, were willing to recognize it as the de facto authority. The result was, however, that the congregation was divided on the most urgent issue of the day and the communion services of the congregation had to be discontinued. It was not until five months later that the wound in the congregation was healed, it being agreed then to forgive the past on both sides and live as formerly. On November 13, 1778, the trombones played for the first time in months to announce the holy communion, at which festival "the gracious presence of the dear Savior was felt by everyone."

Another of the twenty-two who took the oath of allegiance was David Tannenberg, Jr. In his case the act was a matter of patriotism. In April, 1781, much to the consternation of the village elders, David, Jr. allowed himself to be elected a lieutenant in Captain John Smuller's Eighth Company of the Third Battalion of Lancaster County Militia, and in the same year performed a tour of duty in Bucks County. The elders suggested to his father that the son be dismissed from the community and attached to another master outside the village, but Tannenberg admitted that he no longer had sufficient authority over his son to do that. Apparently the father was also somewhat reluctant to lose the services of his apprentice-son. Finally, after David, Jr. had attended an unauthorized party outside the village, the matter was pressed and he was persuaded to leave Lititz. The minutes of the Elders' Conference of December 1, 1781, commemorate his departure: "With thanksgiving to the dear Savior it was remembered that David Tannenberg, Jr. who has gone with Brothers Johann Krause and Gottfried Schultze to Wachovia [the Moravian settlements in North Carolina] is now gone from our neighborhood."[90] The following year he was married to Elizabeth Fuller and settled in Philadelphia, where he established himself as a maker of musical instruments.

The problem with David, Jr. was a deep-seated one. When he had first entered school at Lititz, his teacher had regarded him as one of his best students,[91] but almost every reference to him after that pictures him in trouble. When he was twelve, the officials criticized his being seen with Henry Frey's daughter in their outlot.[92] In 1780 he was not considered suitable for membership in his choir because "he has a very indecent way about him and he runs after the girls."[93] He had been apprenticed to his father and assisted him in the organ work, but there was little work during the war years and there were many other attractions for a young man as the army entered Lititz.

There is the suggestion, too, that the father did not give the kind of direction that he should have, and certainly not the kind that the church officials approved of. More than once he was spoken to about his son's behavior.

> Casslers and Tannebergers allow their sons to develop a World-Disposition, in which they run on the farms and after the girls and are addicted to the clothing-foolishness of the world. And the parents do not punish them or let them be punished. It will be good for some Brothers to speak with the fathers.[94]

On at least one occasion he was also rebuked for giving opportunity for "all kinds of doubtful gatherings" of the neighboring young people.[95] And he was criticized for allowing Tobias Hirte into his home too often, for Hirte was considered to be openly leading the young people into temptation.[96] When Tannenberg drew up his will in 1796, he judged his son to be worthy of an inheritance of only one English guinea,[97] but the faults of the son may well have been born of the laxity of the father.

6

Tragedy and Triumph

There had been little opportunity for organ building during the war. In the five-year period from 1777 to 1781, Tannenberg built only two small organs, one for the Single Brethren's House in Lititz (1777), and a house organ for a gentleman in York, Pennsylvania (1780). Only one other business trip is mentioned, a two-week visit to Bethlehem and Nazareth to repair their organs. Nevertheless, Tannenberg had no thought of abandoning his profession. He resisted the suggestion that his shop be used for quartering army officers during the winter of 1777-78 (Brother Grube complained that Tannenberg had given him difficulty upon difficulty in the matter[98]) and he was reluctant to part with the services of David, Jr. even though there was little organ work and Samuel was now old enough to take his place.

As the war drew to a close, organs were again in demand. In 1782 Tannenberg installed an organ in the Moravian Chapel at Hope, New Jersey, and the following year traveled to Hagerstown, Maryland, with an organ. In 1784 he spent three weeks in York, Pennsylvania, installing an organ in the German Reformed Church. While in York, he visited the Moravian congregation there and on several occasions delivered brief addresses to the Brethren.[99] In 1786 he placed an organ in the union church (Lutheran and Reformed) at Egypt, Pennsylvania.

During these years the Lititz congregation laid plans for a new church building and asked Tannenberg for an organ suited to it. Not only did he construct the organ, but he also played an important part in the planning of the graceful church building itself. As a member of the building committee, Tannenberg prepared a model of a steeple for the church. At first there were objections to it, primarily on the grounds that it would be too elegant for a Moravian church, but finally Tannenberg's model was accepted with the conviction that everyone in the vicinity would be pleased to have a church with such a beautiful steeple in the township.[100] Some years later, when the magnificent steeple of Trinity Lutheran Church in Lancaster, Pennsylvania, was being built, Tannenberg presented a plan for a frame or scaffold to be used in the construction, and his plan was adopted by the vestry.[101] He also designed the pulpit for the Lititz Church and was often consulted by the church officials in building matters.[102]

During these years, also, changes were taking place in the Tannenberg household. On June 30, 1782, Rosina Tannenberg was married to "Billy" Cassler, son of the village tanner and shoemaker, Ludwig Cassler, who had built the first private house in Lititz, next door to the *Pilgerhaus*, Tannenberg's home. On September 24, 1784, Elisabeth Tannenberg married John Schropp, who was for many years the warden at Nazareth and Bethlehem. As the household diminished, and with David, Jr. gone, Tannenberg came to rely upon his son Samuel for assistance in his work and for companionship in his travels. Samuel traveled with him to Hagerstown, York, and Egypt, as well as to Lancaster in 1784, where they spent some time repairing organs in the Moravian, Catholic, and Reformed Churches, and to Philadelphia and Bethlehem in 1785.[103]

But once again the elders were not satisfied with the way Tannenberg was raising his children. When Samuel appeared with a new pocket watch, they solemnly discussed the matter: "That Brother Tanneberger is allowing his son Samuel to buy himself a watch, and is even helping him to do it, is something that can be considered as clothing-foolishness and, as such, cannot be sanctioned."[104] During the war, the elders were concerned that, with no demand for organs, the Tannenberg boys were not learning a trade, and they felt particularly sorry for Samuel because there is ground to fear that, if something is not done about it soon, he may follow in the footsteps of his older brother. Therefore, Brother Horn has been requested to speak with Brother Tanneberger, not to order him, but as a friend in the matter, and if possible to try to bring him to find his son, Samuel, a steady occupation.[105]

Samuel, however, remained an organ builder, even staying with his father a year past his majority without wages in order to learn his trade more perfectly.[106] He grew into a gay young man, well-loved for his "charming manner and his good genius,"[107] and popular among the young people of the vicinity. The elders, however, discerned a worldly disposition in him and refused to consider him a member of the congregation. Then, suddenly, in June, 1788, when he was in his twenty-third year, Samuel was stricken with severe abdominal pains and, within a few days, was dead. It was a deeply saddened father who wrote of the passing of his second son.

> Through the years of his childhood he gave the best hope of success, and was the joy of his parents and almost everyone, in part because of his manner and skill in natural things. The first change and inclination to the world, that we noticed, was at the time that the hospital was here. We often told him of the danger he would come into in this way, but he always answered that he did not know yet what he would choose; there was still time. And so we had to watch his progress with embarrassment, a progress which ended with a painful and swift death . . . . As long as he was conscious [during his illness], he expressed himself sometimes so that one noticed his thoughtfulness. He said to his father: "If I get well again, I will make good use of my time." Question: "But not in a wicked way?" Answer: "Certainly not" . . . From then on he did not seem to be conscious. What may have happened in that time between him and the Savior, only he knows, who sees the heart.[108]

Many people attended the funeral, including many young people from the neighborhood and even from Lancaster. Pastor Klingsohr used the occasion to preach on the necessity of repent-

ance, warning the young people not to wait until their deathbeds
to mend their ways. An unnamed friend placed a long memorial
poem in the Lancaster paper, mourning the loss of Samuel, who
was identified as "a son of the famous organ builder."[109] And
a father grieved, perhaps for the joy of a lost companion, perhaps
at the loss of the one who was to carry on his art, and perhaps,
too, at the unhappy conclusion of his efforts to raise a son.

At the time of Samuel's death, Tannenberg was engaged in
the construction of his greatest work, the organ for Zion Lutheran
Church in Philadelphia. On July 20, 1786, he had met with the
vestry of the church and a contract for the organ had been
signed.[110] After the organ for the Moravian Church in Lititz
was completed in 1787, he began to work on the Philadelphia
organ, apparently spending most of his time for the next three
years in its construction. While much of the organ could be built
in Lititz, there was considerable work to be done in Philadelphia
and Tannenberg spent at least three-and-a-half months there in
the summer and fall of 1790. In August of that year, he wrote
a letter from Philadelphia to Ferdinand Detmers in Lititz which
gives a rare glimpse into his work as well as his piety.

Philadelphia, August 25, 1790

Dearly beloved Brother Detmers,

Hearty greetings to you and to your dear wife. That I
and my assistants are well, I receive with thanks from the
hand of the Savior, and through his blessing we have also
come so far that I hope to be finished with the chest of the
main manual in about two months. Seven stops are ready
now. The pedal is also finished with the exception of the
Posaun Bass, that is to say, five stops [are completed]. The
echo is completely assembled and ready. There is only one
stop in the upper manual, namely the Principal. When everything on the main chest is drawn, together with the pedal,
it already fills the church rather to everyone's astonishment.

A week ago it was very hot here. However, I have been
quite well and with the assistance and blessing of my faithful
Savior I will continue my work until I have completed it.

> Herr Helmuth is already working diligently on the festival
> psalm for the consecration . . . .[111]

Pastor Helmuth had indeed been busy, preparing for the service of consecration, writing verses, translating them into English, and consulting with the organ committee. He was also making arrangements for the visits of President Washington and Thomas Mifflin, the "President" of Pennsylvania. On September 3, Washington visited the church as the organ was played and the children of the church sang for him. Three weeks later, President Mifflin and the members of the Supreme Executive Council of Pennsylvania came to hear the organ. In spite of the satisfaction that these visitors had shown on hearing the organ, Helmuth worried and prayed for the success of the public service to be held on October 10. "The organ, the organ—O dear God, it is consecrated to you. You know that I am anxious about next Sunday and Monday. Lord, have mercy—." Two weeks after the service he was still dreaming about the organ.[112]

In spite of Helmuth's concern and a rainy Sunday, the consecration services were well received.[113] Visitors were utterly amazed at the organ. Built on the same pattern as the organ for Trinity Lutheran Church in Lancaster, it was however larger—twenty-four feet wide and twenty-seven feet high—and was decorated in a unique way. More than a hundred brightly polished pipes were visible in the front of the organ. Above them on the middle tower was depicted the sun, rising out of a bank of clouds and dividing them with its golden rays. On the next towers were gilded eagles flying toward the sun, with the inscription: "They that wait upon the Lord, shall mount up like eagles." On the side towers were two angels, one with the Gospel and the other with the sealed book of the Revelation, both with trumpets in their hands and looking as though they intended to fly up into heaven. Although the basic design was Tannenberg's, the building of the organ case was the work of a local builder, George Vorbach, who was also praised for his work. The spectators were impressed, too, by Helmuth's musical texts, based on the organ's heavenly decorations and sung to organ accompaniment, but Tannenberg himself considered the music to be foolish, and "not according to our [Moravian] taste."[114]

The organ was such an attraction that the services had to be repeated twice that day and once more the following day when the English-speaking community and members of other churches were invited, and then again the next Sunday, not to mention the special service for the President the following January. But the master organ builder took little credit for his work. When he had heard that the pastors and some of the officials of Lititz were coming to Philadelphia for the services, he had written, "I encourage you again to come, not to see anything special, but to share my gratitude that the faithful Savior has so mercifully assisted me."[115]

If there was any danger that the praise given his organ should cause Tannenberg to lose his humility, it must have been overcome by the public announcement, only two weeks after the organ's consecration, of his son's bankruptcy. The Philadelphia *General Advertiser* of October 28 declared that

> a commission of bankrupt is awarded and issued forth against David Tanneberg, junior, late of Easton in the County of Northampton, Musical-Instrument-Maker, Dealer and Chapman; and he being declared a Bankrupt, is hereby required to surrender himself to the Commissioners . . . at the bankrupt office, in the City of Philadelphia.

The career of Tannenberg's grand organ was just as unfortunate as that of his son. On the evening of December 26, 1794, only four years after the organ's installation, fire broke out in the tower of Zion Lutheran Church, someone having carelessly left hot ashes in a wooden container in the vestry room. The fire seemed to burn itself out and the building was thought to be safe, but later it broke out under the roof with flames seen as far away as Woodbury, New Jersey, and the building was burned to the ground. There was an unfortunate lack of water at that location and the crowd, instead of obtaining water, stood by idly watching the building burn. Nothing was saved but some windows and some of the organ pipes. The organ's destruction by fire must have seemed a malicious kind of irony to the Moravian Brethren for, while Tannenberg was in Philadelphia to erect the organ, he had been delegated by the Lititz Brethren to look for a fire engine for their town. He had taken time from his work to price several and had observed a large one, said to be one of the best, standing beside the Lutheran Church.[116]

7

Brother Bachmann

Death visited the Tannenberg household again in 1792 with the passing of Tannenberg's wife, Anna Rosina. She had lived with pleasure in Lititz since their arrival there in 1765 and, in fact, had remarked when she first entered their house that she would like to die there. Now, after some years of illness, she developed dropsy and died early in the morning of February 17, 1792. The members of the trombone quartet climbed to the church steeple and announced with a chorale that there had been a death in the congregation, the people recognizing, from the selection played, that the person who had died had been a member of the choir of married persons. Tannenberg later gave testimony to the congregation that his wife had been a "true soul" and that her heart had belonged to the Savior.[117]

More conscious now of his own mortality, Tannenberg began to search for a partner and possible successor to his art. The training he had given to his sons was to no avail with Samuel dead and David, Jr. exiled from Lititz, and now bankrupt. Indeed, young David's difficulties were not yet at an end. His wife and one of their four children died in the yellow fever epidemic of 1793[118] and he was forced to send the other children to relatives for their care. His son William was sent to Lititz to live with his grandfather where he remained until the elder Tannenberg's death. Perhaps inevitably William, too, fell into disfavor with the town elders and was admonished on several occasions for his conduct and his lack of interest in the Savior or the congregation.[119] David, Jr. remained in Philadelphia, working as a joiner and cabinetmaker. In 1797 he was married to Eva Reimer by the German Reformed pastor.[120] The next year they moved to Montgomery County, Pennsylvania, where he was employed for sixteen months by John and Andrew Krauss, Schwenkfelder organ builders and grandsons of one of Father Klemm's companions on his trip to America.[121] He assisted them with organs for the Reformed Church at Longswamp (later a union church) and the Catholic Church at Goshenhoppen, both in Berks County, Pennsylvania,[122] and then left their employ in the summer of 1799. After that time his whereabouts are not known, but it is known that he died sometime before his father's death in 1804.

The loss of Tannenberg's sons was in part made up for by a local joiner, Johannes Schnell, who had worked as Tannenberg's apprentice since 1786, but it soon became clear that Schnell was not capable of becoming a master builder.[123] Tannenberg then requested permission to send to Herrnhut for someone who could learn his profession, suggesting to the officials that they should be even more concerned than he that his art not be lost to the community.[124] Receiving official permission from Bethlehem, Tannenberg wrote to Brother Johann Philip Bachmann in Herrnhut who, after some delays, set out for Pennsylvania, arriving at Lititz on February 17, 1793. It had been hoped that, when he arrived, Bachmann could marry Tannenberg's youngest daughter, Anna Maria, and the two were married on April 16.[125]

Philip Bachmann had been born in Kreuzburg, Thuringia, in Germany, on April 22, 1762. After learning carpentry from his father, Sebastian (who may also have been a piano builder), he left home in his sixteenth year and came to work for a master who was acquainted with the Moravians. Desiring to become better acquainted with these people, Bachmann visited a Moravian community and, after living in several such communities, arrived finally in Herrnhut. There he learned the manufacture of musical instruments and from there he left to work with Tannenberg.[126]

Bachmann's arrival made it possible for Tannenberg to engage in a large volume of organ work in the last decade of the century. It was a period of extensive church building among the German-Americans and there was an increased demand for new organs.[127] Before Bachmann's arrival, Tannenberg had built organs for Spring City, Pennsylvania, and Graceham, Maryland. Now, with Bachmann's assistance, organs were made during the next eight years for Nazareth, Philadelphia, Lower Heidelberg Township, "Guts'town," Macungie, Lititz, Tohickon, Lancaster, and "Witepain" Township in Pennsylvania, for Baltimore, Maryland, and two organs for Salem, North Carolina. In addition, trips for tuning and repair work were made to Reading, Emmaus, Lancaster, Philadelphia, and Baltimore.

The organs for distant Salem in North Carolina presented a unique challenge to Tannenberg. An organ had been requested by the Moravians in Salem as early as 1794, but because of other work it was not completed until 1798. By that time Tannenberg felt that his age (he was now seventy) would not permit him to make the arduous trip south, and Bachmann was sent to install the organ, leaving Lititz on April 19 and returning on June 16.[128] The next year, a second and larger organ was begun for the new church then under construction in Salem. This time Bachmann was to spend a year in Salem working on the organ, but by the time of his return his relations with Tannenberg would be broken beyond repair.

Several factors led to the rift between the two organ builders. On February 6, 1799, Anna Maria Bachmann had drowned herself in the Lititz stream known as the "Little Spring." The diarist mentions the event only briefly and leaves much to conjecture. "This evening we had a great shock. The married sister Maria Bachmann threw herself into our Creek, where she was soon thereafter found without any sign of life."[129] It has been suggested that she acted out of depression at having no children after six years of marriage. Apparently, there were also rumors about Bachmann's treatment of her.[130] Whatever the reasons for her suicide, her death broke one of the links between her father and her husband.

On December 19, 1800, shortly after returning from his second trip to Salem, Bachmann was married again to Susanna Elizabeth Albrecht, daughter of the Lititz gunsmith. Earlier that year (May 30) Tannenberg, too, had remarried. After five other women had been considered, the one chosen for his second wife was an old acquaintance, Anna Maria Lang, who had already been twice married and twice widowed.[131] Tannenberg maintained afterward that he had remarried mainly to have someone he could trust to care for his affairs if he were to go to Salem, but again he was unable to make the trip.[132] Apparently, Bachmann resented the marriage, perhaps thinking that it would deprive him of his share of Tannenberg's estate when he died. (When Tannenberg did die both Bachmann and Tannenberg's wife quickly entered caveats against the probation of any will until they could be heard in the matter.[133]) Be that as it may, the main cause of the break between the two men was, indeed, money.

Tannenberg's inability to travel to Salem left most of the details concerning their second organ—which he considered one of his most beautiful works—in Bachmann's hands.[134] Even a firm price could not be fixed in Lititz, for much of the work had to be done in Salem with local materials and local labor. Thus Tannenberg was not certain what return he should have gotten for the organ except that he was certain that he had not received enough, nor was he ever able to get an accounting of monies from Bachmann. Bachmann had also displeased Tannenberg in the installation of a rank of pipes which Tannenberg had made for the organ in the Moravian Church in Bethania, North Carolina. Tannenberg complained later that he had not received any money for these pipes.[135] In letter after letter to the Salem authorities, Tannenberg repeated his complaints against Bachmann and his justifications of his own actions, revealing the impatience and bitterness that age and experience sometimes create.

It is hard to avoid the conclusion that Bachmann's character, too, played a part in the difficulties. Bachmann claimed that he was working with diligence, according to his best knowledge and conscience, to complete the organ. At which Tannenberg remarked, "I do not doubt it, for it honors him, which is of great importance to him." Tannenberg added that the installation and tuning take a good deal of time, and require considerable industry and patience "which he often lacks."[136] It appears, too, that Bachmann had been the object of slanderous reports while in Salem, in part because of his wife's suicide. On this point, however, Tannenberg could find no fault, saying only that Bachmann was by nature an outspoken person.[137]

After Bachmann's return from Salem, the dispute came before the church officials. Tannenberg was determined not to give Bachmann any further work and Bachmann had therefore requested permission to establish himself independently in Lititz as an instrument maker. After considering various factors, such as Tannenberg's possible need of help in his later years, but also Bachmann's "uncontrolled manner of thinking and speaking" which had given them a poor impression of him, they decided to consult Tannenberg and, if he had no objection, to allow Bachmann to remain.[138] There was no objection, Bachmann stayed, and the next year was permitted to build his own house in Lititz.[139]

Although the breach between the two men was never fully repaired, there was some further collaboration between them. When Tannenberg's organ for the Lutheran Church in Madison, Virginia, was ready, it was Bachmann who made the trip to install it, and when Bachmann built his first organ after leaving Tannenberg (for the Moravian congregation at Schoeneck, Pennsylvania), Tannenberg made the metal pipes for it.

After Tannenberg's death, Bachmann continued to build organs at Lititz. He is known to have made at least seven organs between 1803 and 1819, in addition to completing the organ of another builder in Philadelphia in 1821. (Bachmann's organs are listed in the Appendix.) After that time, he is said to have turned to fine cabinet work and the building of pianos.[140] One of Bachmann's sons by his second marriage, Ernst Julius, also became an organ builder but, work becoming scarce, he left home to teach school.[141] For more than twenty years prior to his death, Philip Bachmann suffered severely from rheumatism and, especially in the winter, was often confined to bed. From the beginning of the year 1837, he was a complete invalid and he died at the age of seventy-five on November 15, 1837.[142]

When Bachmann had arrived from Germany, Tannenberg's earlier assistant, Johannes Schnell, had been sent to Nazareth to work with Brother William Henry, but by 1795 the organ work had increased to such an extent that he was recalled to assist the two builders at Lititz.[143] While this was helpful to Tannenberg, it was not entirely satisfactory to the community, Schnell's conduct being such that, at one point, the officials were prepared to send him to Salem. Schnell was accustomed to sleeping in Tannenberg's shop, and holding late gatherings there which the elders feared would lead to mischief. Tannenberg was advised to give Schnell a room in his house so that he could see "whether he was in bed at the right time" (Schnell was then fifty-six years old!). Schnell had also been left alone with a single woman in Tannenberg's house while Tannenberg and Bachmann were installing the Whitpain organ, which resulted in a further admonishment to Tannenberg.[144] Nevertheless, Schnell remained in Lititz, assisting Tannenberg, until the latter's death.

With Schnell's assistance, Tannenberg completed three organs in these last years of his life: for New Holland, Pennsylvania, in 1801; for Madison, Virginia, in 1802; and for York, Pennsylvania, in 1804. He had also planned a fine organ for the Moravian Church in Bethlehem, traveling to Bethlehem on horseback in July, 1803, to sign the contract. But he died before work on the organ was begun. When Brother Herbst heard the news of Tannenberg's death, his first thought was, "Now he will build no more organs for Bethlehem."[145]

An earlier trip to Bethlehem had permitted Tannenberg to visit his daughter Elisabeth there shortly before her death on August 23, 1801. Her silhouette, made earlier at Peale's Museum in Philadelphia, shows her to have been an attractive, comfortable, Bürger's wife.[146] With her passing, four of Tannenberg's five children were dead. Only Rosina Cassler survived her father.

8

York

As Tannenberg celebrated his seventy-sixth birthday in 1804, he could look back on a long and fruitful life. He had built or helped to build almost fifty organs of such quality that he was widely recognized as an artist without equal in the nation.[147] With the exception of slight attacks of gout, his health had not interfered with his work until the previous year. Then, in September of 1803, he suffered a stroke. He quickly recovered, but there remained a certain weakness which led him to believe that his earthly pilgrimage was nearing its end.[148]

In spite of his weakness he carried on his work. He had in preparation an organ for the Lutheran Church in York, Pennsylvania, and on April 16, 1804, he left for York to make the installation. The organ had not yet arrived and he used his time to write what may have been his last letter, to John Schropp in Bethlehem.

April 20, 1804

My dearly beloved Brother,

Since I have a good opportunity [to send a letter] through John Hall, I want to inform you of our well being with these few lines, for when we reflect on our age, we can do nothing other than be heartily thankful to the Savior for all the favor and assistance that we enjoy from him each day. I for my part have recovered considerably. Still I feel that I am old and daily grow older. But for all that strength is at hand to proceed with my work. I am waiting now for

the organ to come to Yorktown; it is all packed and I await
the wagon daily. When the organ has been set up, it will
be a weight off my shoulders, until I must take on an even
greater one [the organ for Bethlehem] for which I beg of the
true God and Savior grace, blessing, and assistance.[149]

The organ finally arrived and Tannenberg began the work
of installing it in the gallery of the Lutheran Church. On May
17, toward evening, while he was standing on a bench or scaffold
to tune the organ, he apparently suffered another stroke and fell
to the floor of the gallery, striking his head as he fell. He came
to and was carried to his quarters and it was thought that the
accident was not serious. However, when convulsions set in "it
was suspected that the Savior would use this occasion to call him
home."[150] Later he was able to rest and yielded himself calmly
to the will of God. The next day he spoke often of his good
mother. In the evening strong convulsions returned and as the
end approached, he received the blessing for his homeward journey from Brother Beck. A messenger was sent to Lititz to
bring his wife, but when she arrived at noon on May 19, she was
informed that he had died that morning.

The funeral services were held at ten o'clock on May 21.
One of the largest gatherings that had ever been seen in York
attended the funeral "for he was esteemed and loved by everyone because of his loving and affable conduct." The service itself
was held in the Lutheran Church with the body placed before the
altar and his organ playing for the first time. He was buried in
the Moravian God's Acre as the children of the Moravian and
Lutheran Churches sang hymns beside his grave.[151] One of the
texts was written for the occasion by Ludwig Miller, the Lutheran
schoolmaster:

Ruh sanft!	[Rest gently!
Schlaf wohl in deiner Gruft.	Sleep well in your grave.
Bis dass dein Jesus dich	Until your Jesus you,
Zu gleicher Zeit auch mich	And me at that time too,
Zum Leben wieder ruft.	To live again shall save.
Ruh sanft!	Rest gently!
Schlaf wohl in deiner Gruft.[152]	Sleep well in your grave.]

PART II
THE ORGAN BUILDER'S CRAFT

9

The Conception of an Organ

In an age of electronic organs and of pipe organs ruled by pneumatics and electricity, it may seem that the organ builder's craft as Tannenberg practiced it is worthy of mention only as a historic curiosity. There are, however, a growing number of people who see in the older methods of organ construction classic principles which even today provide the most satisfying organ sounds. One of the first to express this "heretical belief in the beauty of the old organs" was Albert Schweitzer, who expressed his ideas first in 1906 in the book *The Art of Organ Building and Organ Playing in Germany and France*, a book which initiated a new appreciation of the classical organ.[1]

The older organs achieved their beauty through purely mechanical means. The keys were connected by means of an elaborate system of wood strips (trackers) and rollers or squares to valves which admitted air into the windchest. When the valves were opened, air supplied to the windchest at a low pressure entered into channels on which stood pipes of the same note, though belonging to different ranks or stops. When a stop knob was drawn, it moved a slider and allowed the air to enter all the notes of that stop as they were played. The result of these mechanical actions is a precision and clarity of expression and a fullness of tone which is too often lacking in modern organs. Finally, the organs were enclosed in a case which not only added visual beauty to aural, but served as a means of focusing and projecting the

59

Key Action: Key (A) is depressed by player, the tail of the key rising as the front descends. This draws the trackers (B) in the direction of the arrows, the squares (C) transferring the motion from vertical to horizontal to vertical again. The system of trackers and squares is spread from "key scale" (all trackers and squares the same distance apart as the keys) to "chest scale" (all trackers the same distance apart as the note channels in the chest, which is a wider scale) by a rollerboard (D). Tracker (B) above the rollerboard pulls down the note channel valve, called a pallet (E), admitting wind to the note channel and thence to the pipes.

Stop Action: Stop knob is drawn at console, pulling stop-knob rods (F) in direction of arrows. The forward motion of the rod is transferred from the upper to the lower level by the trundle (G). At the lower level it pulls forward the bottom of the rocker (H), causing the top of the rocker to pull in the opposite direction. This in turn places the slider (J) in "on" position. The slider is a perforated strip of wood running between the top of the note channels and the pipe toeboards (K). When it is "on," the holes correspond to the pipe holes and wind may flow into a pipe when the valve below its note channel is opened by the key, causing it to sound.

BARBARA OWEN

A reproduction of the internal mechanism of a Tannenberg organ at Old Salem, N.C. Credit: Old Salem, Inc., Winston-Salem, N.C.

sound into the building, especially when mounted high in the church gallery as was the custom.

It was this classic conception of organ building which Tannenberg learned from Klemm and, through him, from the European masters, and which he brought to near perfection in an American setting. This discussion of the organ builder's craft is not intended as a treatise on classical organ building—that is readily available elsewhere[2]—but rather to demonstrate the way in which Tannenberg expressed some of these conceptions and to depict something of the organ builder's craft as it was practiced in the eighteenth century.

Although there were organ builders who advertised their works in Tannenberg's time—one Johannes Scheible, "organ maker in New Holland" was placing newspaper advertisements as early as 1788[3]—there is no record of Tannenberg's having done so. There was no need for advertisement among the Moravian communities; the constant travel and exchange of documents among the communities gave each a full and detailed knowledge of activities in the whole brotherhood. And as Tannenberg expanded his work among Moravians, it inevitably became known among other religious groups. When Tannenberg installed an organ in the Moravian Chapel in Lancaster in 1765, two members of the German Reformed Church there inspected his work and mentioned that they would like to have one made for their church, which was indeed done in 1770.[4] Once several organs had been placed outside the Moravian communities, the exchange of pastors among the churches spread the knowledge of Tannenberg's work and skill. The pastor who was at Trinity Lutheran Church in Reading, when an organ was bought in 1771, later moved to Frederick, Maryland, and was influential in the purchasing of an organ from Tannenberg in 1775. Likewise, Justus Henry Christian Helmuth, the pastor at Zion Lutheran Church, Philadelphia, when it purchased its famous organ, had previously been at Trinity Church, Lancaster, when its organ was obtained. The glowing newspaper accounts of the Tannenberg organs in the Reformed Church in Lancaster and in Zion

Lutheran Church, Philadelphia, must also have brought further business to the builder.

After a church had decided to purchase an organ, the usual procedure was to take up a subscription toward the cost. Several of the old subscription lists have survived. The one at Zion Lutheran Church, Baltimore, for example, lists fifty-seven subscribers with amounts ranging from three shillings, nine pence to eighteen pounds, fifteen shillings.[5] On the basis of the amount pledged, a committee or individual was then delegated to negotiate with Tannenberg as to the kind of organ he could provide. The day after the subscription had been taken at Graceham, Maryland, Johannes Weller was dispatched to Lititz to negotiate a contract with Tannenberg.[6] But for larger works, the builder usually traveled to the church to inspect the site and make an agreement with the church officials.

As Tannenberg approached the building of a new organ, he did it with both practical and artistic considerations. Foremost among the practical considerations was the space available in the church for the erection of the organ. The smaller organs presented little difficulty, but the larger ones had to be built to fit the space available or, since the organs were often placed in new church buildings, space had to be created for the kind of organ that was desired. The Lititz organ of 1787 was made to fit in a fourteen-foot-high church gallery. The case could be arbitrarily limited to that height, but the larger pipes had to be mitered before they could be used.[7] On the other hand, when a new organ was being planned for Bethlehem in 1803, Tannenberg suggested that the walls of the church be run up four feet higher than originally planned to allow room for the organ that was desired.[8]

He was also concerned that the organ he built be appropriate for the size of the building and that it be compatible with whatever other instruments might be used with it, which was especially important in the Moravian churches with their orchestras and trombone quartets. In organs built for distant places, there was the additional consideration of durability. When the Salem congregation first ordered an organ from Tannenberg, this factor influenced the choice of the organ stops.

We had suggested a Gambe for one register, but he
[Tannenberg] says that this is a very delicate register, that
we would have no one to keep it in order, and might not be
able to use it, and he proposes that we take another register,
the Quinte Dene, which is also very beautiful.[9]

Within these limitations the creation of an organ was an
artistic matter. In 1803, with a lifetime of experience behind him,
Tannenberg laid plans for an organ for the Moravian Church in
Bethlehem. His letters to Bethlehem reveal the artist and craftsman at the height of his ability and may be considered as at least
a part of his matured opinion on the art of organ building.[10]

In reply to a request for his ideas concerning the organ, he
wrote that that would not be difficult since he had been occupied
with the matter for over ten years, already had a conception of it
in his mind and had now begun to make sketches of the windchest
and the internal mechanism. His plan was to place the windchest
for the second manual over top of the first. This was partly for
practical reasons—it would give more room in the gallery for the
pedal work and for the organ pumper—but there were also artistic considerations. He felt that the tone of the upper work would
be much more pleasing in that position, being farther from the
listener, and could also be used as an Echo. And the added height
of the organ case would enhance its beauty, even though it would
be more difficult to construct.

When it came to the disposition of the organ, he had at-
tempted to select the best stops for the size of the building, taking
into consideration the fact that trombones would at times be used
with the organ. The specifications Tannenberg proposed for this
culminating work, with his own annotations, are as follows[11]:

On the main manual:

1. Principal	8 foot		Since we have no mix-
2. Octav	4 foot		tures, such a work
3. Quinta	3 foot		must have these so
4. Octav	2 foot		that the organ has an
			organ tone even in
			such a large building.

5. Viola de Gambe	8 foot	
6. Gedackt	8 foot	These are lovely stops.
7. Floeth	4 foot	

The upper manual:

1. Principal dulcis	4 foot	
2. Flauth Amabile	8 foot	These are lovely
3. Gedackt li[e]blich	8 foot	sounding stops and
4. Floeth	4 foot	pleasing for our
5. Salicional	8 foot	[Moravian] use.
6. Quinta Dehn	8 foot	

Pedal:

1. Violon	16 foot	— This I would like to
2. Sub-Bass	16 foot	make of tin [*Zinn*].
3. Octav Bass	8 foot	It is admittedly a

little costly but is much better than the Posaun Bass since it
always stays in tune.

After the two parties had come to an agreement on the specifications and cost of a proposed organ, a formal contract was prepared. Several of these have survived and, inasmuch as the terms
were generally the same in all of Tannenberg's contracts, the one
made with the German Reformed Church in Lancaster, Pennsylvania, is given here in full.[12]

Disposition of an organ for the Reformed Congregation
in Lancaster, consisting of two manuals and pedal, such work
to contain the following stops or registers, namely:

Upper keyboard:

Principal, of metal	4 foot tone
Flauto Traversa (metal through half the manual)	8 foot
Quinta Tona	8 foot
Hautboy (divided)	8 foot
Floet duo [douce], of wood	4 foot

Lower keyboard or manual:

Principal	of metal	8 foot
Octave	ditto	4 foot
Supper Octave	ditto	2 foot
Quinta	ditto	6 foot
Viol de Gambe	ditto	8 foot
Mixtur	ditto	IV ranks
Grob Gedackt	ditto	8 foot
Klein Gedackt	ditto	4 foot

Pedal:

Supbass	of wood	16 foot
Violon	ditto	8 foot

This is to certify that on this day a contract was made and agreed upon by Wilhelm Bausman, Lorens Marquetant, Wilhelm Busch, and Georg Reits in the name of and for the aforementioned congregation in Lancaster on the one side, and David Tanneberg as the organ builder on the other side; as follows:

The aforementioned David Tanneberg, for and in consideration of the following remuneration, hereby agrees to make, build, and install, in the church of the above-mentioned congregation, an organ of such disposition as agreed above. He is to furnish all necessary materials himself at his own cost, with the sole exception of the organ case, and to construct everything according to his best diligence, experience, and capacity, the stops faithfully according to their particular nature, and along with those stops and work to arrange in the best manner the requisite bellows, of which there must be at least three, their size to be four feet wide and nine feet long. In the same way he is to prepare the keyboards and everything necessary, doing it well and in a durable manner, between now and the first day of July in the year one thousand seven hundred and seventy.

In consideration of the above promises and obligations, the aforementioned Wilhelm Bausman, Lorens Marquetant, Wilhelm Busch, and Georg Reits, in the name of and for the aforementioned congregation, obligate themselves to pay the aforementioned David Tanneberg the sum of two hundred and fifty pounds, Pennsylvania money, according to the following terms, namely: a third part of the above-mentioned sum at the time when the organ work is begun, another third when the work on the organ is about half completed, and the remaining third at the end, when the organ has been installed and completely constructed. N. B. the aforementioned Tanneberg obligates himself to do the installation as well as everything else at his own cost.

The aforesaid parties herewith bind themselves firmly to a sure observance of the aforesaid agreement, etc., and have witnessed the same with their signatures this twenty-seventh day of February in the year of our Lord 1769.

P.S. Notwithstanding the above, the aforesaid congregation shall board the aforesaid Tanneberg during the time he requires to install the organ.

Done in the presence of
    Casper Shaffner
    Eberhart Michael
David Tanneberger

At the end of the contract is a typical receipt given by Tannenberg for payment received.

Received December 5, 1769, the sum of 83 pounds, 6 shillings, and 8 pence, as the first third part payment for the organ, by the terms of the above agreement.

£83 6s. 8d.   Received by me, David Tanneberger.

The churches then, on their part, sometimes appointed a committee to superintend the building of the organ. The Lititz diary records the visit of the "Reformed Church Inspector *(Vorsteher)* from Lancaster along with many other people who were here to inspect the construction of the new organ which Brother David Tanneberger is building for them."[13] Likewise, Trinity Lutheran Church in Lancaster appointed a committee of four, including Pastor Helmuth, as "inspectors" of the work.[14] Tannenberg, on his part, returned to Lititz to begin what one contemporary called "that ingenious business" of organ building.[15]

10

That Ingenious Business

The organs were constructed in a stone shop at the rear of Tannenberg's house.[16] During his first years in Lititz, the work had been done in a large room in the house itself, but about 1771 a shop was erected for this purpose.[17] The smaller organs were completely built here and, when they were finished, were set up and demonstrated, attracting visitors from far and near, before they were transported to their destinations. In the case of the larger works, most of the parts were made in Lititz, but the final assembly and the construction of an organ case were done at the site of the installation.

Over the years Tannenberg employed various assistants or apprentices in his work. Originally, his intention was to use members of his family in the work—and, indeed, both of his sons became organ builders—but the Lititz officials soon made it clear that only the sons could be employed in the business: "May 5, 1766. Brother Danneberger shall not use his girl, whom he is to receive from Bethlehem, in organ building as he had intended."[18] There was, however, no need to employ his daughters; skilled craftsmen were readily available in Lititz or from the other Moravian communities. As early as 1762, while Tannenberg was still in Bethlehem, one Peter Rice came to him from Gnadenthal, near Bethlehem, to learn the trade.[19] In Lititz, the elders often discussed the matter of assistance for Tannenberg and in addition to Johannes Schnell and Philip Bachmann the names of Franz Thomas, Nathaniel Schmidt, Augustus Milchsack, and Joseph Ferdinand Bulitschek appear as persons assisting Tannenberg in his work.[20] Bulitschek is most interesting for, after he left Lititz in 1771, he lived among the Moravians in North Carolina and built two organs for them, one for the Salem Chapel (1772), and an identical instrument for the Bethania Chapel (1773). Both were built with two stops and provision for adding a third. The third stop for the Bethania organ was provided later by Tannenberg and this organ was used continuously until it was destroyed in a fire, November 3, 1942. Bulitschek's main pursuits, however, were as a cabinetmaker and wheelwright. He died in 1801, having left the Moravians in 1792.[21]

In his work Tannenberg could also rely upon the services of the other Moravian artisans. Leather for the organ valves and bellows would have been readily available from Ludwig Cassler, his neighbor, or one of the other village tanners. There were several cabinetmakers and carpenters in Lititz, as well as a blacksmith and a toolmaker.[22] A wide variety of tools was also available; an inventory of tools used by Klemm and Tannenberg at Bethlehem lists five types of saws, ten types of flat planes, twelve types of molding or cornice planes and a large variety of chisels, gouges, rasps, and files.[23] And what was not available in Lititz Tannenberg could easily acquire in his trips to Lancaster, Bethlehem, or Philadelphia.

It was in the actual construction of the organ that the master builder's skill was needed and it was for this that his contemporaries referred to him as "that excellent and ingenious artist" and "a great mechanical genius."[24] The construction of an organ was a detailed procedure involving the making of a windchest with its sliders and valves for each manual or pedal of the organ, from one to five bellows to provide the air and ducts to lead it to the windchests, a rank (set) of pipes for each stop to be set on the windchests, the keyboard(s) and pedal (if there was one), the mechanical connections between sliders and stop knobs and between keys and windchests, and finally the organ case. It was a time-consuming business and Tannenberg's contracts often allowed up to two years for the manufacture of the organs.

Tannenberg's organs were usually constructed with fifty-four notes on each keyboard and twenty-five notes in the pedal. This required the manufacture of fifty-four pipes for each stop in the manual (more if it was a mixture, in which several pipes sound for each note played), and twenty-five pipes for each stop in the pedal. Thus, even a small, four-stop organ might contain 216 pipes while the thirty-four-stop organ for Zion Lutheran Church, Philadelphia, contained almost two thousand.

Some of the organ pipes were made of metal, others of wood. For example, in the 1798 Salem, North Carolina, organ 150 of the pipes were metal and 108 were wood. The metal pipes consisted of an alloy of tin and lead referred to as *Zinn*. In the process of restoring the 1804 York organ and the 1798 Salem organ, analyses of the metal pipes revealed that the metal in the York pipes consisted of 60.54 per cent lead and 38.7 per cent tin with traces of other metals, while the metal pipes at Salem were seventy-five per cent tin.[25] The pouring and forming of the metal pipes was apparently something that Tannenberg alone felt capable of doing. He wrote to Salem that their metal pipes were entirely the work of his own hands, and even when Bachmann built his first organ independently of Tannenberg, the latter made the metal pipes for it.[26]

The wooden pipes were carefully constructed from various kinds of wood in order to achieve the proper quality and tone. The craftsmanship was of the highest order.

> If one wished to display the superb craftsmanship of this artist-mechanic by exhibiting a single specimen of his work among the attractions of some brilliant world's fair, any wooden pipe, taken at random and without comparative selection from any one of Tanneberger's organs would serve the purpose quite as well as any other,—so apparent is the loving care with which each individual "voice" was brought into existence.[27]

The necessity of obtaining good lumber was a constant concern of Tannenberg's, and mention is made of his getting wood from both Bethlehem and Philadelphia.[28] Bachmann went so far as to purchase a sawmill and engage in the lumber business, although he did it without the prior knowledge of the church officials.[29]

After the work that could be done in Lititz was completed, the organ was packed and hauled to its destination. Wagons were readily available for this purpose; Benjamin Franklin had noted that in Pennsylvania almost every farmer had his wagon, and a French traveler observed that frequently from seventy to eighty wagons passed through Lancaster in a day.[30] They were the blue and red canvas-covered Conestoga wagons, prototypes of the familiar covered wagons of the Old West. Hauling the organ was the responsibility of those who were purchasing it and the usual procedure was for one of the church members to offer his wagon and team for the hauling and then be reimbursed by the congregation.[31] Tannenberg was greatly concerned that the delicate organ parts be well packed, protected by straw, and arranged in the wagon so that they would not be damaged in transit.[32]

The installation of the smaller organs was a relatively easy matter requiring little time. The organ for the Single Brethren's House in Bethlehem (1776) arrived by wagon on November 23. On the morning of November 25, Tannenberg arrived and by afternoon had begun the work of setting up the organ. Two days later it was ready and was played for the first time.[33] The installation of the larger organs, however, might require weeks or even months. Tannenberg and his son Samuel required three weeks to install the Reformed Church organ in York, Pennsylvania, in 1784, and Tannenberg and his assistants spent at least three-and-a-half months in Philadelphia working on the organ for Zion Lutheran Church in 1790. During the time that the builder and his assistants were at the church working, board and room were provided by the church, with the treasurer also allowing expenditures for such items as caring for the "Organ Maker's Horse" and providing the builder with rum and "madery" wine.[34]

Two major items in the installation of the larger organs were the placement of the bellows and the construction of the organ case. In the smaller organs the bellows were contained within the organ case, but in the larger organs a place for them was necessary outside the case and also out of the sight and hearing of the congregation. As the organs were most often erected in the church gallery, the usual place for the bellows was overhead in the attic. Here from one to five bellows, each four by nine feet, were erected in sturdy frames. The size of the bellows and the work of installation were so great that—at least at the Lititz and Salem churches—the bellows were left in the attics long after the organs had been removed.[35] At Nazareth the placement of the bellows was unusually troublesome. Consideration was even given to erecting an additional building for them. They were finally placed in adjoining rooms, partly in the warden's residence and partly in the residence of the pastor.[36] The bellows were operated by an organ pumper from the gallery by means of a rope or by treading or, if the bellows were in the gallery, by a handle. As he was behind the organ, there was often a device on the organ with which the organist could signal for more air, but the church histories are full of incidents when the pumper could not be aroused from sleep to conclude a service.

The organ cases in the larger works were of Tannenberg's design, but the cost and labor necessary to construct them were the responsibility of the purchaser, as was the painting of the case. Local craftsmen were employed in this work; one Peter Frick, cabinetmaker, for example, received £160 for making the case in Trinity Lutheran Church, Lancaster.[37]

The added expenditures for hauling, boarding the builder, and constructing the organ case meant that the total cost of the organs was considerably more than the amount Tannenberg received. The total expenditure for the 1793 Nazareth organ was £320 although Tannenberg's price was only £274.[38] It was also customary to make a present to the builder and his assistant, which usually amounted to three to five pounds.[39]

11

To the Glory of God

Not all the early churches had organs or even approved of their use. They had been dismissed as "kists [chests] o' whistles" by some of the Scotch Presbyterians, and many churches went well into the nineteenth century with only a pitch pipe or a bass viol to lead the singing. When an appropriation for an organ in the Williamsburg, Virginia, church was being considered by the Virginia House of Burgesses in 1752, some of the "mountaineers" in the assembly "thought an organ was some strange instrument or Rather Monster and so voted only to have an opportunity of seeing one."[40] But the Germans, when they could afford them, sooner or later acquired organs and gloried in them. To one outsider it seemed as though "they place almost half their devotion" in their organs.[41] Tannenberg's organs were thus prominent features in the churches which had them, often commented on by visitors and treasured by the worshipers.

Joseph Henry Dubbs grew up in the home of a clergyman father who served several German churches including the Egypt Church. His recollections of these churches give us a picture of the setting in which Tannenberg's organs were placed.

> The country churches in which my father preached were . . . of stone, nearly square, with double doors and massive stone steps on three sides. The pulpit was of the "wine-glass" pattern; and had a square wooden table— always called an altar—before it; surrounded by a chancel

railing. Opposite to the pulpit, on the high gallery which occupied three sides of the church, was a good pipe-organ. The church was kept scrupulously clean, and at stated intervals, the floor was adorned with patterns and flowers made with white sand. People who entered the church were careful not to efface these ornaments.[42]

As was the case in these churches, Tannenberg's organs were usually located in the church gallery, most often at the rear of the church, but on occasion on one of the side galleries.

The picture was somewhat different in the Moravian chapels. The Moravian churches also had galleries on which the organs were placed, but the "chapels" were only rooms in a *Gemeinhaus* (congregation house). This building included the pastor's living quarters, rooms for visitors, and a meeting room or chapel *(Gemeinsaal)*. Here there was no gallery and the organ stood among the worshipers. A visitor to Nazareth described the chapel organ in this way: "In front of the President's or minister's chair and table is a large organ within a pew, which surrounds it, and is erected for musicians."[43]

Tannenberg's organs also had to share attention in the Moravian meeting places with the paintings of John Valentine Haidt.[44] Visitors almost invariably were impressed by two things in their visits to Moravian meeting places, the organs of Tannenberg and the paintings of Haidt. John Adams described the Bethlehem meeting place to his wife in this way:

> They shewed Us their Church which is hung round with Pictures of our Saviour from his Birth to his Death, Resurrection and Ascension. It is done with very strong Colours, and very violent Passions, but not in a very elegant Taste. The Painter who is still living in Bethlehem, but very old— he has formerly been in Italy, the school of Paints. They have a very good organ in their Church of their own make.[45]

The organs themselves were fashioned so that they were pleasing not only to the ear but to the eye as well. Tannenberg's graceful organ cases were almost always painted white with gold pipe shades setting off the lustrous natural metal of the exposed pipes, thus creating a modest beauty quite fitting in a place of worship.[46] Two notable exceptions to this color scheme are recorded. During the time that Tannenberg was in Lancaster installing the 1765 Moravian organ, he made a trip to "Shikel's furnace" and, while he was away, Brother Philip Thomas painted the organ dark blue—whether with or without Tannenberg's knowledge is not recorded.[47] And the 1798 organ for Salem, North Carolina, not only was built with an unusual style of case (very similar to contemporary organs in Germany), but was painted to imitate grained mahogany.[48]

The keyboards of Tannenberg's instruments are striking because their colors are the reverse of what is common today in America; the naturals were black and the sharps were white. At the sides of the manual were the stop knobs, and the section with the manual and stop knobs could be closed with small doors, which on the Madison, Virginia, organ can still be locked with an ancient S-shaped key. The smaller organs (sometimes called chamber organs or house organs) had larger doors which enclosed the otherwise exposed pipes, thus giving the whole case something of the appearance of a cabinet or secretary. Another variation in style, found in several of Tannenberg's organs, was the reversed console organ where, in order to give the organist a view of the minister, the console with keyboard and stop knobs (and pedal if there was one) was detached from the case and turned away from it. In this type of organ the seat for the organist was between the case and the console and was raised above the floor with the trackers from the console to the case passing under the organist's feet.

During the nineteenth century, styles changed and many of the organs were painted over in a darker color. The position of the organs was also changed and many were brought down from the gallery to the front of the church. As some of the organs have been restored in recent years, they have been returned to the original color scheme, although it has not been possible to return all of them to the gallery position for which they were originally intended.

The culmination of the process of building and installation
was the public consecration of the organ, when it was first
played publicly and dedicated to the praise and adoration of
God. These were services attended by large crowds of church
members and visitors—almost two thousand were counted at
Lititz in 1787[49]—and long remembered by those who were
there. "This day," reads the record of Zion Lutheran Church,
Spring City, Pennsylvania, "next to the day when the church
was consecrated, was the most eventful in the history of the
congregation," and the Hebron Moravian diarist wrote in a
similar vein: "Since the founding of the Hebron congregation,
there has been no day like this."[50] There were, after all, few
good organs in these country regions, and few festive occasions
for amusement. But even in the larger cities the consecrations of
Tannenberg's organs were momentous events. The consecration
of the 1799 organ in the Lancaster Moravian Church was duly
noted in a newspaper with the unlikely name of *Der Deutsche
Porcupein (The German Porcupine)*.[51]

> Last Sunday, the twentieth of this month, was the con-
> secration of the new organ in the church of the United
> Brethren, made by the celebrated artificer David Tanneberg
> in Lititz. The musicians and trombonists from Lititz came
> the day before and the trombonists entertained the inhabitants
> on Saturday evening by playing some tunes from the tower of
> the Lutheran Church, which produced universal pleasure.
> The day of consecration will certainly remain in the memory
> of everyone who participated. The morning and afternoon
> services were each musically opened and closed with a suitable
> Biblical text. During the time in between, the trombonists
> again played some tunes from the tower of the Reformed
> Church. They concluded in the evening, in harmony with
> the organ in the Lutheran Church [Tannenberg's organ of
> 1774], in the presence of a large crowd of people. And thus
> was this day concluded with praise and gratitude to the Lord.

In light of the present interest in ecumenicity, the involve-
ment of various denominations in the consecration services de-
serves to be mentioned. Both the Lutheran and Reformed

Churches in Lancaster had Tannenberg organs at that time and thus would have had a special interest in the services, but this was not a singular occurrence. The consecration of the 1787 Lititz church and organ was attended by "esteemed persons of all the religious organizations and denominations in Lancaster and Lancaster County," leading a reporter to wish that all the defenders and advocates of religious tolerance in Germany could have been there to see how all the Christian religions and sects had attended together, with the greatest harmony and affection.[52] At other services of consecration, ministers of various denominations took part in leading the public worship or shared in the preaching.[53]

The Moravian musicians were also frequent participants in the services. The musicians often traveled from one of their communities to another for such services, and they were also invited outside the Moravian communities to participate in church or organ dedications of various denominations. The musicians contributed to the services in various ways. The consecration of the 1782 Hope, New Jersey, chapel and organ was announced early in the day by the sound of trombones and the procession from the old chapel to the new one was made to the accompaniment of the trombones.[54] At Nazareth in 1793, not only were the Nazareth and Bethlehem musicians present to render a concert, but the texts of the songs had been printed in Easton and were distributed to the guests.[55] On at least one occasion Tannenberg himself lent his musical ability to the consecration service. He was present when the Graceham, Maryland, organ was consecrated in a communion service and was moved by the occasion to sing a few suitable verses from the gallery, much to the Brethren's pleasure.[56]

Among the Moravians, love feasts and communion services were often included in the consecration services. The love feasts were fellowship meals, usually of coffee and buns, distributed and eaten in the church in a service which consisted largely of song. At the consecration of the Salem Church organ in 1800, one thousand buns were baked to be served with beer at a love feast after the consecration, but the crowd was so large—almost two thousand attended—that the buns had to be cut in two to serve everyone.[57] On the more practical side, most of the churches, Moravian and non-Moravian alike, used the occasion and the presence of visitors to take up a collection toward the cost of the organ.

Tannenberg's relation to the organs did not necessarily end with their installation and consecration. In many cases he returned to tune or repair the organs at a later date. There were also organs of other builders and imported organs which he was called upon to tune or repair. Many of the earlier American organs had been imported but always with the risk of having no one to repair them. Indeed, one Virginian had objected to the importation of an organ because "experience had informed us that these instruments could not stand long in this Country. Dust, Spiders, and dirt daubers would Stop up all the Pipes, and when it should be out of Repair, what artificer had we to mend it."[58]

The tuning of an organ was no less important than its building or its playing. It was Albert Schweitzer's opinion that

> good tuners should be paid like ministers, and should occupy such a place in the rank of artists that one artistic tuner should be considered equal to six average *virtuosi,* since a half dozen of the latter are easier to find than one artistic tuner. . . . The work of the tuners . . . edifies generation after generation.[59]

Tannenberg was of the opinion that a new organ should not be tuned again for some time until the woodwork was thoroughly seasoned. He allowed the Lititz Church organ to remain for over seven years without tuning, explaining that a new work changes a good deal in the beginning as the wood dries out.[60] In 1802 he sent the Salem Church directions for the tuning of an organ which have survived and show the details of his work. He was reluctant to have an inexperienced tuner work on the organ and elaborated the dangers of shortening the pipes and ruining the intonation, but there was no longer any possibility of his traveling there to do the work, and he shared his method with the Salem Church.[61] Tannenberg, however, built better than he knew and the Salem organ like many of the "stout old Tanne-bergers" survived the hand of many tuners and may yet be played again.

PART III
THE ORGANS

12

The Measure of the Work

Unfortunately, Tannenberg left no list of the organs which he had built. Nor have any account books been found from which such a list could be reconstructed. In his will, written in 1796, he declared his intention to leave "all my tools, together with all my papers and writings relative to the making of organs, etc."[1] to Philip Bachmann. However, even if they were available to his son-in-law after the broken relations between the two men, which seems unlikely, they have not been found. The only account which is available is a single sheet of paper listing the places for which Tannenberg built organs, with their prices, during the last nine years of his life.[2] It has been necessary, therefore, to reconstruct a list of Tannenberg's organs from many sources with the knowledge that a complete list may never be possible.

Paul E. Beck, relying primarily on records in the archives of the Lititz Moravian congregation, compiled in 1926 a list of thirty-one Tannenberg organs, in addition to one built with Klemm.[3] Through the use of other sources, particularly materials in the Archives of the Moravian Church in Bethlehem, Pennsylvania, a more complete list has been assembled and is presented here.[4] Tannenberg built a total of at least forty-one organs. Five additional organs were built by Klemm and Tannenberg between 1758 and 1762 and are included here to give a complete picture of Tannenberg's work. Two other organs, which are thought by some to be by Tannenberg, are also discussed—an organ for the Reformed Church in Frederick, Maryland (1770), and the Whitefield House organ—as is the proposed Bethlehem organ which Tannenberg did not live to complete. It should be noted, too, that Tannenberg also supplied substantial parts of organs built by others, for example, a third rank for Bulitschek's organ in Bethania, North Carolina, in 1800, and all the metal pipes in Bachmann's 1803 organ sold to the Moravian congregation at Schoeneck, Pennsylvania.

Tannenberg's organs are listed below in chronological order using, where they are available, the dates of their installation or consecration. Where possible, the church or individual which purchased the organ is identified, specifications of the organ are given, and something of the later history of the organ is sketched. For some of the organs the cost is available and is also included, the amount being that paid to Tannenberg, rather than the total cost which was sometimes considerably larger. The prices were consistently given in Pennsylvania currency, using pounds rather than dollars. These prices provide helpful clues to the size of the organs where the organ specifications are not available. Thus, for example, the 1786 organ for Egypt, Pennsylvania, which cost £145 must have had about six stops since the 1791 organ at Spring City, Pennsylvania, which has six stops, cost £150. However, in making such comparisons, fluctuations in the value of the pound must be taken into consideration. In 1771 Tannenberg sold an eleven-stop organ for £230; in 1804 a similar organ cost £355.

Not a few of Tannenberg's organs were used into the twentieth century and parts of still others were incorporated into later organs and survived in that way into this century. But then, Albert Schweitzer said that the sturdy old tracker action organs "will not suffer even when the world comes to an end, but will remain standing there for the angels at the last judgment to play the *Gloria* on."[5] Eight Tannenberg organs are known to exist today (nine, if the Whitefield House organ is his), awaiting the hand of the angels. There are also three surviving Tannenberg cases. The extant organs and cases are marked below with asterisks.

Following the list of organs is an account of several other musical instruments which Tannenberg is known to have made.

13

The Klemm-Tannenberg Organs

1758. Nazareth, Pennsylvania. For the chapel of the Moravian congregation, located in Nazareth Hall.

The organ was first played on August 26, 1758, for a church conference and was used in the Hall until 1793.[6] In that year Tannenberg built another organ for the Nazareth congregation to replace the 1758 organ. The older work was then sold to the Moravian congregation at Emmaus, Pennsylvania, for £30 and moved there in January, 1794. Three months later, Tannenberg arrived unexpectedly in Emmaus to tune the organ for them.[7]

1758. Nazareth, Pennsylvania. For Nazareth Hall.

This was a smaller organ (*positive*) for another room in Nazareth Hall. It was first played on December 24, 1758, to accompany the Christmas songs.[8]

1759. Bethlehem, Pennsylvania. For the chapel of the Moravian congregation.

Klemm and Tannenberg brought the organ to Bethlehem on January 29, 1759, and it was played for the first time that evening.[9] A visitor to Bethlehem in 1799 described the organ in this way:

> The organ in the gallery, is placed contiguous to the wall, and the organist is seated in the front, with the keys before him, and his face toward the congregation. The wires and communications with the pipes pass under his feet, secured by the platform, which elevates him a few inches.[10]

This was the organ that was heard and admired by many other visitors to Bethlehem, especially during the Revolution. It served the Bethlehem congregation until a new church was erected in 1806 and a new organ, built by John Geib of New York City, installed in it.[11]

1760. Christian's Spring, Pennsylvania. For the chapel of the Moravian congregation. Christian's Spring was a small Moravian settlement west of Nazareth and approximately nine miles north-northeast of Bethlehem.

The organ was set up in the new chapel early in July and both were consecrated at a service on July 10, 1760.[12]

1762. Bethabara, Forsyth County, North Carolina. For the chapel of the Moravian congregation.

This small, one-rank organ was taken from Bethlehem, Pennsylvania, to North Carolina by a group of Moravian settlers led by Pastor Johann Michael Graff. The group left Bethlehem on April 20, 1762, for a sea journey, the baggage including the organ having been shipped by way of Easton at the same time.[13] Brother Graff set the organ up in the chapel at Bethabara on July 8, 1762, when it was first played for an evening song service.[14]

This little chamber organ was the first organ in use among the North Carolina Moravians and one of the first in the whole South. As such it aroused the interest of various visitors. In 1767 Governor William Tryon and "his lady" visited the village and remained an hour in the chapel listening to the organ. In 1774 several Indians on their way to Williamsburg attended the evening meeting. The diarist recorded that "the Indians wondered much at the organ, thinking it must be alive if it could make a sound like that; [the organ case had to be opened for them, for they had heard children were inside, who sang]." [15]

The records do not indicate where Graff obtained the organ but, since he had previously been living in the Bethlehem-Nazareth area and in view of the scarcity of organ builders at that time, it seems likely that the organ was the work of Klemm and Tannenberg.

The organ was used in Bethabara until 1798 when it was transferred to the Single Brethren's House in Salem. In 1824 it was again moved to the Moravian Church in Friedberg, North Carolina, where it was used until about 1900.[16]

14

The Tannenberg Organs

1765. Lancaster, Pennsylvania. For the chapel of the Moravian congregation. Cost: £50.

Tannenberg was in Lancaster from April 20 to May 6, 1765, during which time he installed the Moravian organ. On April 22, with one stop of the organ playing, it was used for the first time in the evening song service.[17]

1765 or 1768. York, Pennsylvania. For the chapel of the Moravian congregation.

Consecrated at the Christmas Festival in 1765 (the year is somewhat uncertain), this organ consisted of three stops: an open diapason, flute, and principal. It may also have had pedals.[18]

1766. Philadelphia, Pennsylvania. For "a man in Philadelphia."

The diary of the Philadelphia Moravian congregation for October 29, 1766, records that "Brother Tanneberger returned to Lititz, after he had set up an organ which he had made for a man here in the city." No further identification of the organ's purchaser is given.[19]

1767. Albany, New York.

Tannenberg left Lititz on September 14, 1767, for Albany with a newly completed organ and returned on November 6.[20] The Moravian diaries give no indication of the church for which the organ was intended. However, there was a German Reformed Church in Albany at least as early as 1772 which was provided with an organ, "the first one known to have been used in a church in Albany." It seems likely that this was the church which purchased Tannenberg's organ. The builders of the Reformed Church in Albany were never paid, the congregation was dispersed, and the building was sold about 1794.[21]

1768. Maxatawny, Pennsylvania. For the Lutheran Church (now St. John's Church, Kutztown, Berks County, Pennsylvania).

Tannenberg traveled to Maxatawny with his new organ on November 22, 1768.[22] This was a Lutheran congregation near present-day Kutztown which at a later date shared a building with a German Reformed congregation in what was called a "union church." These congregations erected a new building in Kutztown in 1791 and the organ is said to have been in use there until about 1910.[23] It was, however, extensively remodeled in the 1870s by Samuel Bohler.

As several of Tannenberg's organs were placed in union churches, it should be noted that this was a rather common arrangement among German Lutheran and Reformed congregations in colonial days which has not yet entirely disappeared. The two congregations shared one building for reasons of economy. The building was then alternately occupied by the two congregations. One who grew up in this kind of church in the nineteenth century wrote of it:

> Beyond a few matters of ritual, there was in those days no practical difference between the two denominations, and there was no disagreement. The Lutheran pastors were my father's [the Reformed pastor] intimate friends, and often came to see him.[24]

1769. New Goshenhoppen, Pennsylvania. Near East Greenville, Upper Hanover Township, Montgomery County. For the German Reformed Church.

On October 21, 1769, Tannenberg returned from a six-week trip, during which he had installed an organ in the New Goshenhoppen Church and then repaired the two organs in the Moravian Church in Philadelphia.[25]

There are conflicting accounts of the later history of the organ. One says that it was sold in 1890 to a church in Ohio.[26] Another says that it was dismantled about 1869 and that many of the parts were used in a later organ which was in the New Goshenhoppen Church until October, 1917.[27] In any case, the rounded tops of the towers from the old organ case are still to be seen in the church, set into the wall above the gallery doors on either side of the present organ.

1770. Moselem, Pennsylvania. For Zion (Moselem) Lutheran Church, Richmond Township, Berks County.

This, the oldest of the existing Tannenberg organs, was used constantly from the time of its dedication by the Rev. Johann Helfrecht Schaum[28] in 1770 to its replacement in 1957 by an electronic organ.

Originally it was situated in the rear gallery with its two large bellows on top, just below the rafters and out of the view of the congregation.[29] In 1894 it was rebuilt by Samuel Bohler of Reading,[30] who added a new keydesk and one stop. The organ, however, has its original case, pipes, and windchest and now stands prominently, but unfortunately mutely, in the front of the church. The organ has one manual with the following stops as they are now designated:

1. Sw. Principal
2. 4 foot Flute
3. Sw. Fifteenth
4. 8 foot Violin [added by Bohler]
5. Tremolo [probably also a Bohler addition]
6. 3 foot Twelfth
7. 8 foot Flute
8. Sw. Open Diapason

1770. Frederick, Maryland. For the German Reformed Church.

The histories of the Reformed Church in Frederick state that an organ was purchased for the church from Tannenberg at

---

* Asterisks indicate still-existing organs or organ cases.

a cost of $193.37, which was used by the congregation until 1840.[31] The original church records, however, cast some doubt on this assertion.

The records, while they do contain a list of contributions toward a parsonage and an organ in 1770, indicate that this was for *old* debts. Thus it seems likely that an organ had been in the church prior to this time. Moreover, Tannenberg's name appears only in connection with *repairing* and *setting up* the organ in 1770, and not with its purchase.[32] While it is possible that the organ had previously been purchased from Tannenberg, there is no evidence that he was its builder.

1770. Lancaster, Pennsylvania. For the German Reformed Church. Cost: £250.

The officials of the Reformed Church in Lancaster signed a contract with Tannenberg on February 27, 1769, for an organ with fifteen stops. (The original contract with specifications is included above in Part II, Chapter 9.) The organ was installed in 1770 and first played publicly on December 23, 1770, accompanied by a variety of vocal music composed for the occasion.[33] The organ was replaced in 1885 by a Durner organ, but the original Tannenberg case was retained for the new organ.[34] The case, somewhat enlarged, is still in the church, housing now an electronic organ. As late as 1928, the pipes of the Tannenberg organ were stored in the church, but they have since disappeared.

1771. Reading, Pennsylvania. For Trinity Lutheran Church. Cost: £230.

The date of the organ's installation is not recorded, but the contract made in October, 1769, specified that it was to be set up for use by September 1, 1771. There were to be two bellows, a "handsome case," and the following stops[35]:

Manual:

1. Principal		8	foot
2. Viola de Gamba	(metal)	8	foot
3. Gedact	(wood)	8	foot
4. Flauto Traver	(wood)	8	foot

5. Octave	(metal)	4	foot
6. Super Octave	(metal)	2	foot
7. Fifth	(metal)	3	foot
8. Gemshorn	(metal)	4	foot
9. Mixture	(metal)	3	foot
Coupler with pedals			

Pedal:

1. Sub-bass	(wood)	16	foot
2. Octave	(wood)	8	foot

Tannenberg repaired the organ in 1777, 1789, and again in 1794, when it was transferred to the congregation's new church building. There it served until 1873 when it was sold to a congregation at Tinicum, Bucks County, Pennsylvania, and dedicated there in a special service on November 29, 1873. There are no records concerning the organ at either of the Tinicum churches (Upper Tinicum and Lower Tinicum) but an aged member of the Lower Tinicum Church at Pipersville recalls having played such an organ in that church prior to a fire in May, 1907, which destroyed the church and its entire contents.[36]

1772. —————————————

In the diary of the Lititz Moravian congregation is found this entry for July 31, 1772[37]:

> Several eminent persons from Lancaster were here, among them Doctor Kuhn [Adam Simon Kuhn, elder and trustee of Trinity Lutheran Church, Lancaster] and the English clergyman Barton [Thomas Barton, rector of St. James' Episcopal Church, Lancaster], to see and hear Brother Tanneberger's newly made organ. They were very pleased with it and expressed their gratitude to the musicians [who had performed for them].

Unfortunately, the diary does not indicate the place for which the organ was made.

1773. Lebanon, Pennsylvania. For the chapel of the Hebron Moravian congregation, located in South Lebanon Township, near the city of Lebanon. Cost: £45.

On September 3, 1773, Brother Bader, the pastor at Hebron, visited Lititz and while there examined an organ that

Tannenberg had built.[38] Later that month, two Hebron Brethren were appointed to go to Lititz and negotiate for its purchase. It was offered to them for £45 and the purchase was approved by the congregation. Tannenberg and one of his sons brought the organ to Hebron on Thursday, November 11, 1773, and the next day began to set it up in the second-floor chapel of the stone *Gemeinhaus*. The organ was consecrated on Sunday, November 14, in the presence of a crowd of people from the town and countryside so large that, although extra benches had been provided, the chapel could not contain everyone. In this service the organ was accompanied by violinists from the congregation.[39]

As the first organ in the Lebanon Valley, Tannenberg's work continued to arouse great interest among the people. During the Revolution, army officers often visited the chapel in order to hear the organ. The Hessian prisoners at Lebanon and Hebron, some of whom were confined in the Moravian congregation's building, also showed considerable interest in this instrument.[40]

In 1847 the congregation, with its organ, moved into Lebanon. There, between two and three o'clock on the morning of July 29, 1858, both church and organ were destroyed by fire.[41]

1774. Lancaster, Pennsylvania. For the Lutheran Church of the Holy Trinity.

In 1771 Trinity Church opened a subscription for a new organ and appointed a committee to superintend its building, specifying that the organ was to have no more than twenty stops.[42] The contract was made with Tannenberg, who installed the organ in 1774. Services of consecration were held on December 26 of that year. The Lititz diarist recorded the event in this way:

> December 26, 1774. Today the new organ, which Brother Tanneberger has built in the Lutheran Church in Lancaster, was consecrated. It has twenty stops. Doctor Kuhn kindly invited our trombonists to play a few tunes in their worship service, which under such agreeable conditions could not be refused.

Five of the Brethren accordingly went that day with hautboys and trombones and played in two preaching services to the great satisfaction of the people.[43]

In 1854 the Tannenberg organ was replaced by one made by Henry Knauff of Philadelphia. He had examined the old organ the year before and declared that it was so completely worn out that any further repairs on it would be useless. The congregation agreed to purchase a new organ from Knauff but would allow no more than fifteen hundred dollars for it. Knauff replied that that amount would be adequate only if he could use the old case and some of the pipes.[44] Thus, through the parsimony of the church officers, the magnificent Tannenberg case was preserved. When the Knauff organ was replaced in 1887, the case was again retained, but was enlarged by an additional tower and flat at either end. In this condition it still graces Trinity Church, although the organ itself has since been replaced twice more.

1775. Lancaster, Pennsylvania. For St. Mary's Roman Catholic Church.

The Catholics in Lancaster erected a very graceful stone church in 1762. A Tannenberg organ dating from 1775 was used in the building,[45] but no details of its construction or history are now available.

1775. Frederick, Maryland. For the Evangelical Lutheran Church. Cost: £400.

In 1779 the pastor of the Lutheran Church at Frederick wrote an account of the improvements in the church during the eight years of his ministry there. Among them was the purchase of "a beautiful new organ built at a cost of £400."[46] He did not mention the date of its installation, but the Moravian diarist at Graceham, Maryland, noted that Tannenberg and his son had visited there November 25-26, 1775, on their way home from Frederick, where they had installed an organ.[47]

The Frederick organ was used until 1855 when it was thought to be beyond repair and was sold.[48]

1776. Easton, Pennsylvania. For the Lutheran and Reformed congregations.

Tannenberg left Lititz on September 9, 1776, for Easton where he was to install a new organ.[49] It was soon placed on the west side gallery of the new union church building of the Lutheran and Reformed congregations in Easton and was presumably dedicated along with the building on November 17, 1776.[50] In this place Tannenberg's organ was a not altogether silent witness of the events of the war which had already begun.

Early in 1777 a treaty was made in Easton between several representatives of the Continental Congress, the Pennsylvania Assembly, and the Council of Safety of Pennsylvania on the one side and a number of Indian chiefs, representing the Six Nations and their confederates, on the other, the colonists hoping to prevent an alliance of the Indians with the British. "The German Church being most convenient to hold the treaty in, the same was readily granted by the congregation. . . ." The secretary of the American Commissioners—none other than Thomas Paine, the author of *Common Sense*—duly reported the daily ceremonies that accompanied the treaty making.

> The ceremony of shaking hands being gone through, a glass of rum was served round to all the Indians present, and the health of the congress and the Six Nations with the allies were drank. The organ being ordered to play in the mean time.
>
> [Then, at the end of the day] a glass of rum each was served round, pipes of tobacco lighted and smoked—organ played—adjourned to next day at noon.[51]

The organ had the following stops[52]:

1. Gedakt	8	foot
2. Principal	8	foot
3. Salicional	8	foot
4. Principal	4	foot
5. Flute	4	foot
6. Super Octave	2	foot
7. Quinte	3	foot
8. Mixture		

1. Four-stop Tannenberg organ built for the Moravian congregation in Graceham, Maryland, in 1793. It is now located in the church parlor of the Single Brethren's House at Lititz, Pa. Credit: Lititz Moravian Archives Committee, Lititz, Pa.

2. Organ built by Tannenberg in 1798 for the chapel of the Salem Moravian congregation. It is now in the Moravian Single Brethren's House at Old Salem, North Carolina. Credit: Old Salem, Inc., Winston-Salem, N. C.

3. Harpsichord made by Johann Gottlob Klemm in 1739, now in the Metropolitan Museum of Art, New York. The inscription on this only surviving work of Klemm reads: *Johannes Clemm fecit Philadelphia 1739.* Tannenberg learned the craft of organ building from Klemm. Credit: The Metropolitan Museum of Art. Rogers Fund, 1944.

4. The chapel of the Moravian Single Brethren's House as it has been restored in Old Salem, North Carolina. The 1798 Tannenberg organ was built originally for the chapel of the Salem Moravian congregation. As in many of the Moravian chapels, a painting by John Valentine Haidt (Mary with Jesus and John the Baptist) shares prominence with Tannenberg's organ. Reproduced by courtesy of Old Salem, Inc., Winston-Salem, N. C.

5. The Moravian Church in Lititz, Pennsylvania. Tannenberg not only built an organ for the church but also designed the pulpit and the church steeple. The church was destroyed by fire in 1957 but has been rebuilt according to the original design. Reproduced by courtesy of John Morman, assistant headmaster, Linden Hall School for Girls, Lititz, Pa.

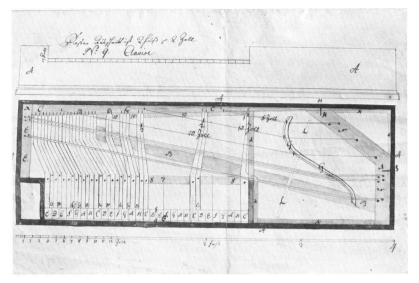

6. Drawing of a clavichord sent by Tannenberg to the Moravian officials at Salem, North Carolina, with instructions for building the instrument. In addition to the organs, Tannenberg built at least one clavicembalo and two pianos. Credit: The Moravian Music Foundation, Winston-Salem, N. C.

7. Early view of the *Pilgerhaus* (center), Tannenberg's home in Lititz. Built by George Klein, the town's founder, in 1754, it was the first house in Lititz and served as the congregational meeting place as well as a tavern and store before Tannenberg purchased it in 1765. Credit: The Archives of the Moravian Church, Bethlehem, Pa. From a drawing by Nicholas Garrison, Jr. (1757).

8. Oldest of the existing Tannenberg organs. It was built in 1770 for Zion (Moselem) Lutheran Church, Richmond Township, Berks County, Pennsylvania. In 1894 the organ was rebuilt and a new keydesk was installed, but the original case, pipes, and windchest were preserved. The organ is the only one designed by Tannenberg with triangular towers. Credit: Zion (Moselem) Lutheran Church, R.D. #3, Kutztown, Pa.

9. Close-up of the 1793 Tannenberg organ built for the Moravian congregation in Graceham, Maryland. Reproduced by courtesy of Grant Heilman, Lititz, Pa.

10. Title page of the program for the service of consecration for the organ (the largest one Tannenberg built and his masterpiece) in Zion Lutheran Church, Philadelphia, Pennsylvania, October 10, 1790. Another service was held in January, 1791, with President Washington in attendance. Credit: The Archives of the Ministerium of Pennsylvania at the Lutheran Theological Seminary, Philadelphia, Pa.

11. Six-stop Tannenberg organ in Zion Lutheran Church, Spring City, Pennsylvania. The organ is played once each year in a special service on the Sunday nearest the anniversary of the organ's first use on October 9, 1791. Reproduced by courtesy of Zion Lutheran Church, Spring City, Pa.

12. Tannenberg's daughter "Liesel" (Maria Elisabeth) from a silhouette made at Peale's Museum in Philadelphia, Pennsylvania. She was the wife of John Schropp who was for many years the Moravian warden at Nazareth and Bethlehem. Credit: The Archives of the Moravian Church, Bethlehem, Pa.

13. Case of the organ built by Tannenberg in 1770 for the German Reformed Church in Lancaster, Pennsylvania. Now somewhat enlarged, the original case houses an electronic organ. Credit: First Reformed Church of the United Church of Christ, Lancaster, Pa.

14. Letter in German written at Lititz, Pennsylvania, on September 23, 1794, by David Tannenberg to his son-in-law and daughter, John and Liesel Schropp. The letter shows Tannenberg's early concern for a new Bethlehem organ which he finally contracted for in 1803 but did not live to complete. Credit: The Archives of the Moravian Church, Bethlehem, Pa.

15. Tannenberg organ built for Trinity Lutheran Church, Lancaster Pennsylvania, in 1774. Probably by the time the picture was made, the organ works had already been replaced by Henry Knauff, but Knauff retained the Tannenberg case and some of the pipes. The original organ case is still in the church although it has been enlarged by the addition of an extra tower and a flat at either end. Reproduced by courtesy of the Evangelical Lutheran Church of the Holy Trinity, Lancaster, Pa.

16. Watercolor of David Tannenberg (left) installing his last organ in Christ Lutheran Church, York, Pennsylvania. The self-taught artist, Lewis Miller, was the son of Ludwig Miller, the schoolmaster of the Lutheran Church in York. Courtesy of The Historical Society of York County, York, Pa.

17. Organ built in 1773 by Joseph Bulitschek for the Moravian Parish House chapel in Bethania, North Carolina. Tannenberg supplied one rank of pipes for the organ. Earlier, Bulitschek had worked as Tannenberg's assistant in Lititz. Credit: Old Salem, Inc., Winston-Salem, N. C.

18. Four-stop organ now in the Whitefield House, Nazareth, Pennsylvania. Although it is thought by some to be the first organ (1746) used by the Moravian Church in Bethlehem, Pennsylvania, it is in the Chippendale style of the late eighteenth century and closely resembles the 1793 Tannenberg organ made for Graceham, Maryland (illustration No. 1). The organ may well have been made by Tannenberg for one of the Choir Houses at Bethlehem. Credit: The Moravian Historical Society, Inc., Nazareth, Pa.

19. Organ made by Tannenberg and Bachmann for Home Moravian Church, Salem, North Carolina, in 1800. In 1913 the organ was dismantled and is now in storage at Old Salem. Credit: Old Salem, Inc., Winston-Salem, N. C.

20. Tannenberg's last organ, made for Christ Lutheran Church, York, Pennsylvania, in 1804. Tannenberg died while installing the organ and it was played publicly for the first time at his funeral. The organ is now in the Museum of the Historical Society of York County, York, Pennsylvania. Credit: The Historical Society of York County, York, Pa.

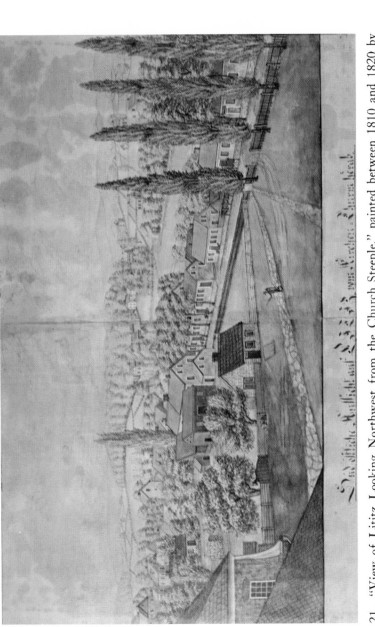

21. "View of Lititz Looking Northwest from the Church Steeple," painted between 1810 and 1820 by Samuel Reinke. Tannenberg's two-story house (center, partially hidden by trees) is north of the main street and west of the alley. Tannenberg's shop is behind the house, with only the roof showing. Reproduced by courtesy of the Lititz Historical Foundation, Lititz, Pa., from an original watercolor owned by the Lititz Moravian Congregation.

In 1831 the union arrangement was dissolved and the building and organ became the sole property of the Reformed congregation. Two years later the organ was sold to the Plainfield Reformed Church (now St. Peter's, near Pen Argyl, Northampton County, Pennsylvania). In 1852 it was repaired by Charles Hanzelman of Allentown, Pennsylvania. The original keyboard was taken out and a reversed keyboard substituted. In 1900 the organ was rebuilt by Lewis B. Clewell of Bethlehem. After these alterations it could still be said that "the wind chest, six sets of pipes, and the handle which pumps the bellows" remained from the original organ. The organ was finally replaced in 1925. Forty-three wooden pipes from this instrument are now on display in the museum of the Northampton County Historical and Genealogical Society in Easton.

1776. Bethlehem, Pennsylvania. For the chapel of the Moravian Single Brethren's House. Cost: £60.

On the same day that the Easton church and organ were dedicated, Brothers Bonn and Benzien left Bethlehem for Lititz to pick up a new organ for the chapel of the Single Brethren's House in Bethlehem. They took with them their old chapel organ, for which Tannenberg allowed £10 toward the cost of the new organ. Tannenberg arrived in Bethlehem on November 25 to set the organ up, and it was played for the first time on November 27.[53]

The Moravian buildings which housed the Single Brethren (as also those for the Single Sisters) included not only living and working quarters, but in each case also a *Saal* or room set apart for the worship services of that choir. It was in the *Saal* that Tannenberg's organ was placed.

1777. Lititz, Pennsylvania. For the chapel of the Moravian Single Brethren's House. Cost £50.[54]

A harpsichord had been used in the chapel of the Lititz Single Brethren's House as early as 1768,[55] but there is no mention of an organ prior to 1777. Tannenberg's organ was set up on August 29, 1777, and played for the first time the following day on the occasion of the close of the Single Brethren's "choir year." [56]

1780. York, Pennsylvania. For Mr. Fischer.

In the fall of 1780, the Moravian Bishop John Frederick Reichel and his wife and Christian Heckewelder journeyed from Salem, North Carolina, to Lititz. On October 25 they arrived at York, Pennsylvania, where they found David Tannenberg engaged in installing an organ. Their travel diary for that date contains this entry:

> We reached Yorktown about two o'clock and were most lovingly received by Brother and Sister Neisser . . . . Toward evening Brother Neisser took Brother Heckewelder to call on Brother David Tanneberger, who has come here from Lititz to set up a beautiful new organ for Mr. Fischer, and we enjoyed seeing this truly handsome work. [57]

"Mr. Fischer" was presumably John Fischer, a German immigrant who lived in York from about 1756 until his death in 1808. He was a clockmaker by trade, as well as a wood-carver and portrait painter, and was regarded as one of York's "substantial citizens." [58]

1782. Hope, Warren County, New Jersey. For the chapel of the Moravian congregation.

Tannenberg arrived in Hope with their new organ on October 9, 1782. The organ, which is referred to as a small one, was installed in the congregation's new chapel and both were consecrated on November 8. [59] The village of Hope was abandoned by the Moravians in 1808, but the original *Gemeinhaus* in which the chapel was located, is still standing.

1783. Hagerstown, Maryland.

On June 21, 1783, Tannenberg and one of his sons left Lititz for Hagerstown to install an organ there. [60] Recent efforts to determine for whom the organ was built have proved unsuccessful, but it was probably for either St. John's Lutheran Church in Hagerstown or St. Peter's (Beards) Lutheran Church near Hagerstown, both of which had organs at an early date.

1784. York, Pennsylvania. For the German Reformed Church.

Tannenberg and his son Samuel were in York from August 17 to September 7, 1784, setting up and tuning an organ which he had made for the German Reformed Church.[61] The organ, with its universal language of music, must have been a welcome sound to President Washington when he visited this church on Sunday, July 3, 1791. As he wrote in his diary,

> There being no Episcopal Minister present in the place, I went to hear morning service in the Dutch reformed Church—which, being in that language not a word of which I understood I was in no danger of becoming a proselyte to its religion by the eloquence of the Preacher.[62]

The church and the organ were destroyed by fire on July 4, 1797.[63]

1786. Egypt, Pennsylvania. Whitehall Township, Lehigh County. For the Lutheran and Reformed congregations. Cost: £145.

The union church at Egypt dedicated a new church building on June 4, 1786, and about that time a Tannenberg organ was installed. This church, like several others which had organs at a time when most churches did not, was known in the vicinity simply as "the Organ Church." In 1870 the organ was replaced by another built by Charles Hanzelman of Allentown, Pennsylvania.[64]

*1787. Lititz, Pennsylvania. For the Moravian Church. Cost: £200.

When the new Lititz Church was being planned in 1786, Tannenberg advised that an organ suitable to the size and proportion of the building should contain ten or twelve stops, two manuals and a pedal, and he proposed to build such an organ for £350.[65] The church officials in Bethlehem, however, insisted that no more than £200 be spent for an organ,[66] and the organ as built contained only one manual and pedal and these stops:

Manual:

1.	Principal	4 foot
2.	Principal Discant (through three octaves)	8 foot
3.	Viola da Gambe	8 foot
4.	Quintadena	8 foot
5.	Flaut Amabile	8 foot
6.	Floet	4 foot
7.	Octave	2 foot
	Coupler	

Pedal:

1. Subbass
2. Octave Bass

The console of the organ was reversed.[67]

The new church and organ were consecrated on August 13, 1787.[68] The organ was used until 1879 and the next year was transported to the Moravian Church in South Bethlehem, Pennsylvania, where it was used until 1910. Again it was taken down and returned to Lititz.[69] The organ was never set up again, but was stored in the attic of the Single Brethren's House, where it still remains. The bellows, however, had been left in the attic of the Lititz Church and were destroyed with the church in a fire in the summer of 1957. Only recently, plans have been made for the restoration of the organ.

1790. Philadelphia, Pennsylvania. For Zion Lutheran Church. Cost: £1500. After the loss of the organ the newspaper accounts referred to its cost as £3500. This, however, included the cost of the woodwork and the gallery on which the organ stood.[70]

The contract for this, Tannenberg's largest organ, was signed in Philadelphia on July 20, 1786. The organ was completed in the fall of 1790 and public services of consecration were held on October 10 and 11 of that year.[71] The program printed for these services includes these specifications:

Main Manual:

1.	Principal	8 foot	6.	Trumpete	8 foot
2.	Quintaden	16 foot	7.	Octave	4 foot
3.	Gambe	8 foot	8.	Quinte	3 foot
4.	Gemshorn	8 foot	9.	Octave	2 foot
5.	Gedackt	8 foot	10.	Flöte	4 foot

11. Mixture IV to VI ranks

Upper Work:

1.	Princip. dulc.	8 foot	6.	Nachthorn	4 foot
2.	Quinta dena	8 foot	7.	Solicet	4 foot
3.	Vox Humana	8 foot	8.	Hohlflöte	2 foot
4.	Flöte amab.	8 foot	9.	Cimbel	IV ranks
5.	Gedackt	8 foot	10.	Fistel quint	3 foot

Echo—to Tenor F:

1.	Dulcian	8 foot	5.	Fistula oct.	4 foot
2.	Flöt Traver	8 foot	6.	Nachthorn	4 foot
3.	Rohr Flöt	8 foot	7.	Echo Bass	8 foot
4.	Hautbois	8 foot			

Pedal:

1.	Principal Bass	16 foot	4.	Subbass	16 foot
2.	Posaune	16 foot	5.	Octav Bass	8 foot
3.	Quinta	6 foot	6.	Octave	4 foot

In addition to the thirty-four stops, there were also a cymbal star *(Cimbel Stern)*, tremolo, stop valve *(Sperr Ventill)*, and two couplers. The organ was supplied with five large bellows.[72] A set of bells was also to have been included in the organ, but it is not clear whether that was ever done.[73]

This splendid instrument was short-lived. It was destroyed with the church in a fire on December 26, 1794. Some of the organ pipes were saved and were used in the Lowe organ which was installed in the rebuilt church.[74] In 1795 Tannenberg had visited Philadelphia to discuss the rebuilding of the organ, but the contract was given to Lowe.[75]

1791. Spring City, Pennsylvania. East Pikeland Township, Chester County. For Zion Lutheran Church. Cost: £150.

In 1790 Zion Church ordered a Tannenberg organ which was installed the following year and consecrated on October 9, 1791. The church was often thereafter referred to as "the Organ Church."[76]

The organ was in constant use until 1912, when it was replaced by another instrument, but it has been kept in the church and is played once each year in a special service on the Sunday on or nearest October 9, the anniversary of the organ's first use. In 1953 the case and keyboard were returned to their original appearance, while an electric blower was substituted for the original bellows.

The six stop knobs on this one-manual organ presently bear these titles:

1. Dulciana	8	foot
2. Hohl Flote	4	foot
3. Principal	8	foot
4. Octav	4	foot
5. Gedakt	8	foot
6. Super Octav	2	foot

1793. Graceham, Frederick County, Maryland. For the Moravian Church. Cost: £65 to £70.

The members of the Graceham congregation subscribed £65 toward a new organ on Sunday, May 27, 1792, and one of their members left the next day for Lititz to contract with Tannenberg for the organ. Tannenberg arrived to install the organ on April 25, 1793, and it was played for the first time on May 4 in a communion service. It was used again the following day in a preaching service with many neighbors in attendance.[77]

The organ served the Graceham congregation well into this century. In recent years it was restored and moved to Lititz where it has been set up in the church parlor in the Single Brethren's House. The organ has a compass of fifty-four notes and contains four stops. It can either be pumped with a foot pedal to the right of the player or the bellows can be drawn by a second person with a strap at the left of the organ.

1793. Nazareth, Pennsylvania. For the chapel of the Moravian congregation, located in Nazareth Hall. Cost: £274.

By 1792 the organ which Klemm and Tannenberg had made for the Nazareth congregation in 1758 was no longer adequate. (It had also been damaged by unsupervised children playing on it!) Tannenberg agreed to make a new organ similar to the one in the Lititz Church and he and Bachmann took the completed organ to Nazareth on November 12, 1793. It was consecrated on December 15 and played in a public concert the next day.[78]

The organ had one manual and pedal with these stops:

Manual:

1.	Principal	(metal)	4 foot tone
2.	Viol da Gamba	(metal)	8 foot tone
3.	Quintatoen	(metal)	8 foot tone
4.	Suboctav	(metal)	2 foot tone
5.	Floet Amabile		8 foot tone
6.	Floet Douce		4 foot tone
7.	Grob Gedackt		8 foot tone

Coupler (connecting the bass of the manual with the pedal)

Pedal:

1.	Octav Bass	16 foot tone
2.	Subbass	32 foot tone

The Quintatoen, Grob Gedackt, and Subbass ranks were stopped pipes. The console was reversed.[79]

The organ was later transferred to a new church building and then was rebuilt in 1898. In 1913 a new organ was installed. However, the original Tannenberg case was retained and is still in use, as are three of the original Tannenberg stops.

By 1795. Philadelphia, Pennsylvania. For the German Reformed Church.

The Moravian historian Abraham Ritter, writing in the nineteenth century, described the Reformed Church as it was in 1795 and mentioned the organ that was then in it:

> The pedestal pulpit was at the centre of the south wall, the long side of the church; and the organ, a dignified affair,

and monument of Tannenberg's skill, answered from its
elevation—at the touch of a junior Rev. Beebighaus—the
commands of the venerable pastor.

Tannenberg belongs to history as *the* organ builder of
his day, and one of renown . . . . His diapasons were particularly dignified, whilst his upper work, 12th, 15th, and sesqui-
altera, gave brilliancy to the whole.[80]

In 1790 the church council acted to remove the "crown"
which adorned the organ and replace it with a "federal eagle."
This small, gilded, wooden eagle, still in the possession of the
church, is all that remains of the Tannenberg organ. When a new
church building was being planned in 1836, a contract was made
with Knauff to build a new organ for which he was to receive
$2,100 in addition to the old organ.[81]

1795. "Guts'town."

Tannenberg and Bachmann returned to Lititz on August 12,
1795, "from Guts'town, where they had set up an organ."[82]
With only this information, it has not been possible to determine
where the organ was taken, or even with certainty that it was a
new organ rather than a previous organ installed in a new location, since the records usually refer to a *new* organ as such.

*1795. Lower Heidelberg Township, Berks County, Penn-
sylvania.* For St. John's (Hain's) German Reformed Church.

Hain's Church purchased a new organ from Tannenberg in
1795; (it has also been dated 1789).[83] It had eight stops, one of
which was a three-rank mixture, and a white case with unpainted
metal pipes. The organ was remodeled in 1878 by Thomas
Dieffenbach and used until 1904 when a new organ was made by
E. E. Palm of Mt. Penn, Pennsylvania. However, much of the
old organ was used in building the new. In this way parts of the
original Tannenberg organ survived until 1930 when the Palm
organ was disposed of, parts of it being sold to members of the
congregation as souvenirs.

1796. Baltimore, Maryland. For Zion Lutheran Church.
Cost: £375.

Zion Church began a subscription for a new organ early in 1795. The organ was ordered from Tannenberg. Toward the end of the year, he was in Baltimore with the organ, although the work may not have been completed until 1796.

Philip Bachmann came to tune the organ in 1798. Then in 1808 it was transferred to a new church building and at the same time adorned with wood carvings. The church and organ were destroyed in a fire on March 30, 1840.[84]

1797. "Macungie," Pennsylvania. Weisenburg Township, Lehigh County. For Ziegel Union Church, Lutheran and Reformed, located about sixteen miles northwest of Allentown. Cost: £400.

The Macungie or Ziegel Church dedicated a new building in the fall of 1796. In October of the following year, a new Tannenberg organ was installed on the gallery to the right of the pulpit.[85] Local tradition has it that the organ was built by the Lutheran pastor, Johann Friederich Obenhausen.[86] However, the Lititz records indicate that it was a Tannenberg organ.[87] It is possible that Obenhausen negotiated the purchase of the organ, or even that he assisted in the carpentry work on the case as Tannenberg usually left this to others on his larger organs. The organ was later replaced by one built by Charles Hanzelman, probably in 1863-64 when a new church building was erected, and certainly by 1884.[88]

1798. Tohickon, Pennsylvania. Bedminster Township, Bucks County. For the Lutheran and Reformed congregations (now St. Peter's United Church of Christ and Peace Lutheran Churches). Cost: £200.

The organ was installed by February of 1798, for the Schwenkfelder organ builder John Krauss recorded in his diary on February 19, 1798: "I, Andrew [his brother], and Andrew Yeakle went to the Church near Tohiccon where we took a view of that organ."[89]

In 1839 this same Andrew Krauss, with another brother, George, contracted to remodel the organ, adding, among other things, a pedal, a new windchest, and "suitable wings on both sides." The latter, decorative, additions to the case are visible in an existing photograph of the remodeled organ.[90] The organ continued in use until 1918.

1798. Salem (now Winston-Salem), North Carolina. For the chapel of the Moravian congregation. Cost: £150.

As early as 1794 the Salem congregation had written to Tannenberg concerning a new organ but, because of the press of other work, it was not delivered until 1798. In that year it was installed by Philip Bachmann and played for the first time in a song service on the evening of May 22. The organ was used in this chapel and in a later chapel until 1864 when it was placed in storage.

In 1964 the organ was restored by the McManis Organ Company and is now located in the chapel of the Single Brethren's House in Old Salem, the restored Moravian community. The one manual, reversed console organ has a compass of fifty-four notes and contains these stops:

1. Gedackt   8 foot
   54 stopped wood pipes (pipes shorter than one foot of walnut)
2. Principal   4 foot
   54 open pipes of 75% tin (23 of them in the case)
3. Flauto   4 foot
   54 open wood pipes, treble pipes walnut
4. Quinte   2-2/3 foot
   54 open metal pipes
5. Terzian (TC)   1-3/5 foot
   42 open metal pipes

A sixth stop knob reads *Luft* (air) and was originally a signal for the organ pumper. The pitch of the restored organ is about A-430.[91]

1798. Lititz, Pennsylvania. For the chapel of the Moravian Single Sisters' House. Cost: £50.

This small organ was set up July 10, 1798, and consecrated on July 26 by Brother Johannes Herbst with both Tannenberg and Bachmann present. That date was also the thirteenth anniversary of the consecration of the Sisters' House and the services included a love feast, the communion, and the presentation of a "Psalm" prepared by Brother Herbst for the occasion.[92]

1799. Lancaster, Pennsylvania. For the Moravian Church. Cost: £260.

When the Moravian congregation was planning for a new organ in January, 1798, Tannenberg offered to build one with six stops for £180.[93] Specifications for the completed organ are not available, but the higher price finally paid would indicate that it was larger than originally planned. The organ was dedicated on Sunday, January 20, 1799, with the assistance of musicians, singers, and trombonists from Lititz.[94]

1799. "Witepain" Township, Pennsylvania. For St. John's Lutheran Church, Center Square, Whitpain Township, Montgomery County. Cost: £200.

The organ was consecrated in the Lutheran Church on September 8, 1799.[95] In 1834 a new stone church was built and the organ placed in the rear gallery. Here it served until "it became suddenly and hopelessly silent at a Sunday morning service in 1888." The following year it was dismantled and the various parts sold at auction to the members of the congregation.[96] Today there reside in the safe of St. John's Church two small wooden pipes, the last mementos of Tannenberg's work.

*1800. Salem (now Winston-Salem), North Carolina. For the Moravian Church. Cost: something more than £400. Tannenberg received this amount but insisted that he had not received all that was due him. The total cost to the Salem congregation, including hauling, lodging for Bachmann, etc., was £794 9s. 10d.[97]

When what is now called "Home Church" was being planned in Salem, an organ of two manuals and pedal was ordered from Lititz. The main parts of the organ were made in Lititz by Tannenberg, but Bachmann also spent about a year in Salem working on the organ. There being a difference of opinion about where to place the organ in the church, lots were used, and the

one drawn read, "The Savior approves that plans be made to place
the organ in the new church in the gallery on the steeple side."
The church with its new organ was consecrated on November 9,
1800.[98]

The stop list is as follows:

Great Organ (54 notes):

1. Open Diapason	8 foot	5. Principal	4 foot
2. Flauto	4 foot	6. Fifteenth	2 foot
3. Stopped Diapason	8 foot	7. Twelfth	3 foot
4. Gamba	8 foot	8. Viola	8 foot

(The Viola was a later addition.)

Swell Organ (54 notes):

1. Salicet	4 foot	4. Flauto Amabili	8 foot
2. Open Diapason	8 foot	5. Piccolo	2 foot
3. Flauto Douce	4 foot	6. Viol Di Gamba	8 foot

Pedal (25 notes):

1. Violonalto	8 foot	2. Bourdon	16 foot

Couplers:

Great to Pedal; Swell to Pedal; Swell to Great

The organ had a reversed console and also a nagshead
swell for the enclosed upper manual division, a mechanism first introduced only ten years earlier in England. The organ was reno-
vated in 1910 by S. E. Peterson, when keyboards with modern
colors were substituted for the originals. The organ was used
until 1913. It was then dismantled and is now in storage at Old
Salem.[99]

1801. New Holland, Pennsylvania. For St. Stephen German Reformed Church. Cost: £200.

A new church building was erected for the German Reformed Church of New Holland in 1801 and on September 19 of
that year a Tannenberg organ was consecrated with the assistance
of the Moravian musicians from Lititz.[100] Early in its history the
organ was damaged by vandals who removed and partly destroyed some of the organ works[101]; nevertheless, the organ was

used by the congregation until 1920. In 1920 a new organ was obtained and the old one, still serviceable, was given to the recently organized German Reformed Church in Lititz, with a feeling of fitness that it was being returned to the place of its origin. There it was stored in the basement of the home of the Reformed pastor, George B. Raezer. Due to a disagreement with a builder who was to repair the organ, it was never used, but remained in the pastor's basement, from which it finally disappeared.

The organ had one manual and ten stops. It was also equipped with a foot lever which brought into play the Open Diapason stop, and another which withdrew it.[102]

1802. Madison, Virginia. For Hebron Evangelical Lutheran Church. Cost: £200.

The legend of the old organ in Hebron Church was that it had been the gift of the King of Sweden, made at Lutzen, shipped to Philadelphia, and then hauled by wagon to Virginia. The fact is that the organ was made at Lititz by David Tannenberg, taken by wagon from there by members of the Lutheran congregation, and installed by Philip Bachmann.[103] The exact date of its installation is not known, but Bachmann returned from Virginia about December 1, 1802.[104]

The organ has been in constant use since that date and is practically unaltered from its original condition. In recent years it has been cleaned and restored to its original appearance and has served as a valuable guide in the restoration of other Tannenberg organs, notably the 1798 Salem, North Carolina, organ.

The one-manual organ has a pitch of A-430 and contains the following stops[105]:

1. Principal Dulc.   8 foot
   54 metal pipes, 1-12 quintadena basses
2. Gedackt   8 foot
   54 stopped wood pipes
3. Octave   4 foot
   54 open metal pipes
4. Flute   4 foot
   54 open wood pipes

5. Quinte   2-2/3 foot
   54 open metal pipes

6. Octave   2 foot
   54 open metal pipes

7. Terzian   1-3/5 foot
   54 open metal pipes (rank breaks back to 3-1/5 foot at
   Mid. C)

8. Mixture   III (1-1/3 foot)
   162 open metal pipes

1804. York, Pennsylvania. For Christ Lutheran Church.
Cost: £355.

Tannenberg installed this, his last organ, in April and May,
1804. While working on the organ, he suffered a stroke, fell from
a bench or scaffold, and died on May 19. His funeral service was
held in the Lutheran Church on May 21, 1804, with the organ
playing for the first time in his honor.[106]

The organ was used in two successive church buildings until
1893 when a new organ was obtained. Later the Tannenberg organ was moved into an adjoining chapel. About 1910 the organ
was somewhat altered by Reuben Midmer of New York. The
voicing was loudened, the wind pressure raised, and the pedal
stops converted to pneumatic action. In 1945 it was given to the
Historical Society of York County, located in York. The organ
was reconditioned in 1959 by Fred Furst of York and is now in
the museum of the Historical Society. E. Power Biggs has said
that this organ "quite leads the procession in tonal character and
excellence" among the American organs he has played.[107]

The organ was originally purchased with a legacy from a
church member and an inscription on the organ reads (in German), "A Legacy from Widow Barbara Schmidt." The one-
manual and pedal organ has the following stops[108]:

Manual (54 notes):

1. Open Diapason	(metal)	8 foot
2. Stopped Diapason	(metal)	8 foot
3. Dulciana	(metal)	8 foot
4. Octave	(metal)	4 foot

5. Melodia (listed as Oboe 8 foot)		4 foot
6. Nazard	(metal)	2-2/3 foot
7. Fifteenth	(metal)	2 foot
8. Sesquialtera		II ranks
9. Trumpet	(metal)	8 foot
Coupler		

Pedal (25 notes):

1. Bourdon	(wood)	16 foot
2. Open Diapason	(wood)	8 foot

Proposed Organ for the Moravian Church in Bethlehem, Pennsylvania.

When the Moravian congregation in Bethlehem was planning a new church building in 1803, they turned to Tannenberg for a new organ. Although his death the following year prevented the completion of the organ, a contract had been signed and the specifications of what was to have been a major work are of interest. The organ was to have had two manuals and pedal with the following nineteen stops:

Main Manual:

1. Principal (of good English tin)		8 foot
2. Viola di Gamba	(metal)	8 foot
3. Gross Gedackt (wood in bass, metal in treble)		8 foot
4. Quintaden	(metal)	8 foot
5. Oboe	(metal)	8 foot
6. Gemshorn	(metal)	4 foot
7. Flaute	(wood)	4 foot
8. Principal octav (of English tin)		4 foot
9. Principal	(metal)	2 foot

Upper Manual:

1. Principal dulcis (of English tin)		8 foot
2. Salicional	(metal)	8 foot
3. Bourdon or lieblich Gedackt	(wood)	8 foot
4. Flauto amabile	(wood)	8 foot
5. Rohr Floethe	(metal)	4 foot
6. Salicet	(metal)	4 foot

Pedal:

1. Octav Bass	(wood)	8 foot
2. Subbass	(wood)	16 foot
3. Violon Bass	(metal)	16 foot
4. Posaunen Bass	(wood)	16 foot

There were to be two couplers and a reversed console. The work was to cost between £700 and £800.[109]

The Whitefield House Organ.

In the Whitefield House in Nazareth, Pennsylvania—once the "Nursery" where Tannenberg and Klemm lived for a time, and now the Library and Museum of the Moravian Historical Society—there is a small four-stop organ which may be one of Tannenberg's works. The organ was obtained from the Moravians in Bethlehem and has been reputed to be the first Bethlehem organ, purchased from Klemm and Hesselius in 1746. The claim, however, seems doubtful.

The 1746 Bethlehem organ was replaced by a Klemm-Tannenberg organ in 1759. At that time the older organ was taken to Nazareth, perhaps for repairs or temporary use there.[110] Then, in 1761, the Bethlehem diary records that their former chapel organ was taken to Lititz and installed in the Moravian chapel there by Tannenberg.[111] The transfer of the 1746 organ to Lititz has not been generally known and tends to discredit the claim of the Whitefield House instrument to be the original 1746 organ.

In addition to these facts, it has been pointed out that the Whitefield House organ is made in the Chippendale style of the *late* eighteenth century and that it bears a striking resemblance to the 1793 organ which Tannenberg made for the Moravian congregation at Graceham, Maryland (now at Lititz).[112] It is quite possible that the Whitefield House organ was also made by Tannenberg, perhaps for one of the Choir Houses at Bethlehem, and would thus be one more work to be credited to the master builder.

15

Other Tannenberg Instruments

In addition to making and repairing organs, Tannenberg gave some time and thought to the manufacture of other musical instruments. On June 29, 1789, one Jeremy Elrod returned to Salem, North Carolina, from a trip to Pennsylvania, bringing with him a clavicembalo (a kind of harpsichord) which Tannenberg had made for the chapel of the Single Sisters' House in Salem.[113] There are also, in the archives of the Moravian Music Foundation, directions for making a clavichord, with an accompanying drawing, which Tannenberg had sent to Salem from Lititz.

The authorities at Salem also asked Tannenberg to make them a piano *(Clavier)*, which he was not able to do because of other work.[114] Tannenberg, however, is known to have made at least two pianos which he sold for twenty-two pounds, ten shillings each. One of these was made for "Brother Lembke" and the other for the "Kinder-Haus," the Lititz school now known as Linden Hall.[115]

APPENDIX

BACHMANN ORGANS

The following is a list of organs known to have been built by Johann Philip Bachmann from the time of his separation from David Tannenberg to his death in 1837.

1803. Schoeneck, Northampton County, Pennsylvania. For the Moravian congregation. Cost: £65.

This organ, for which Tannenberg made the metal pipes, is said to have been made originally for the Indian Mission on the Muskingum River in Ohio. Since there would be no one there who could repair it, the organ was made as durable as possible. It had three stops, was enclosed in a yellow case, and had a black cloth curtain in front. The organ was never sent to the Ohio Moravians but was sold to the Schoeneck congregation and consecrated there in a service on January 23, 1803. Some years later it came into the possession of the Bethlehem Theological Seminary.[1]

1805. Hanover, Pennsylvania. For Emmanuel German Reformed Church.

The organ had eight stops, two of wood and six of metal, and two large bellows. It was used until 1887 and then was given to a mission church of the Reformed denomination in Marietta, Pennsylvania, where it was in use until at least 1909.[2]

1808. Lebanon, Pennsylvania. For "Old Salem" Lutheran Church.

This was a two-manual organ.[3]

1810. Jonestown, Lebanon County, Pennsylvania. For Zion Lutheran Church. Cost: $811.04½.[4]

1813. Hamburg, Berks County, Pennsylvania. For St.
Michael's Union Church, Lutheran and Reformed. Cost: nearly
$1,100.[5]

1818. Harrisburg, Pennsylvania. For Zion Lutheran
Church. Cost: $1,400.

In August, 1814, a committee of the church went to Lititz
to negotiate a contract for the organ. There was some delay in
its construction, the matter was renewed in 1816, and the organ
was finally installed in May, 1818. The church was destroyed in
a fire on October 21, 1838.[6]

1819. Myerstown, Lebanon County, Pennsylvania. For
Friedens Lutheran Church. Cost: $800.[7]

This one-manual and pedal organ was used until 1904 when
it was moved to Luther Memorial Church in Tacoma, Washington, and used there until Easter, 1933. Then it was completely
rebuilt but the organ case and the eight-foot Diapason pipes were
retained in the new instrument. The case was originally white but
was later finished in a dark color. The specifications of the organ
before it was rebuilt were[8]:

Manual (54 notes):

1. Diapason	8 foot
2. Stopped Diapason	8 foot
3. Quintadena	8 foot
4. Octave	4 foot
5. Harmonic Flute	4 foot
6. Twelfth	2-2/3 foot
7. Fifteenth	2 foot
8. Mixture	III ranks

Pedal (18 notes):

1. Bourdon	16 foot

1821. Philadelphia, Pennsylvania. For St. John's Lutheran
Church.

A large organ was begun in St. John's Church by Matthias
Schneider in 1818 but was not completed. On May 18, 1821,
Bachmann signed a contract to complete the organ on or before
August 1 of that year.[9]

NOTES

PREFACE

1. Washington's visit is mentioned in Jacob Cox Parsons (ed.), *Extracts from the Diary of Jacob Hiltzheimer of Philadelphia, 1765-98* (Philadelphia: William F. Fell and Co., 1893), p. 166. The poem and reference to Washington's first visit are from the diary of Justus Henry Christian Helmuth for August 17 and September 3, 1790. The diary is located in the Archives of the Ministerium of Pennsylvania at the Lutheran Theological Seminary in Philadelphia.

2. *Neue Philadelphische Correspondenz,* No. 4, October 12, 1790.

PART I

1. Georg Neisser, *A History of the Beginnings of Moravian Work in America* (Bethlehem, Pa.: Archives of the Moravian Church, 1955), p. 61.

2. Edmund DeSchweinitz, *The Life and Times of David Zeisberger* (Philadelphia: J. B. Lippincott and Co., 1870), p. 13.

3. The information concerning David Tannenberg's parents is from their memoirs, preserved in the Archives of the Moravian Church at Bethlehem, Pennsylvania. Some details are also taken from Georg Neisser, "A list of the Bohemian and Moravian Emigrants to Saxony . . ." in *Transactions of the Moravian Historical Society,* Vol. IX, Nos. 1-2 (1913), *passim.*

4. See Georg Neisser, *A History of the Beginnings of Moravian Work in America* (Bethlehem, Pa.: Archives of the Moravian Church, 1955), pp. 64-65; and Vernon H. Nelson (ed.) and Carl John Fliegel (trans.), *Christian David: Servant of the Lord* (Bethlehem, Pa.: Archives of the Moravian Church, 1962).

5. See August Gottlieb Spangenberg, *Leben des Herrn Nicolaus Ludwig Grafen und Herrn von Zinzendorf,* II Band (Zu finden in den Brüdergemeinen, 1773), pp. 1071-72.

6. Most of the details of Tannenberg's early life are from his two memoirs: one, apparently written about 1750 (now in the Archives of the Moravian Church at Bethlehem), and a second, written about 1790 and circulated at the time of his death. Several copies of the latter have been located, one in the Bethlehem Archives (made from a copy in Germany) and two in the archives of the Lititz Moravian Church.

7. Spangenberg, *op. cit.,* pp. 1309-32.

8. *Ibid.,* III Band, pp. 1759-68.

117

9. Letter from Tannenberg to Zinzendorf, November 15, 1751. A copy of the letter is in the Library of Congress (Archiv der Brüderunität, Herrnhut, Rep. 14A, No. 30, Letter 89).

10. John W. Jordan, "Moravian Immigration to Pennsylvania, 1734-67" in *Transactions of the Moravian Historical Society*, Vol. V, No. 2, pp. 54, 66-69. See also Joseph Mortimer Levering, *A History of Bethlehem, Pennsylvania, 1741-1892* (Bethlehem: Times Publishing Co., 1903), pp. 233-34.

11. Two memoirs of Anna Rosina Kern Tannenberg have been located, one in the Archives of the Moravian Church at Bethlehem, and a longer and presumably later one in the archives of the Lititz Moravian Church.

12. Herbert H. Beck, "Town Regulations of Lititz" in *Historical Papers and Addresses of the Lancaster County Historical Society*, XXXIX (1935), 114.

13. Benjamin Franklin, *The Autobiography of Benjamin Franklin* (New Haven: Yale University Press, 1964), p. 237.

14. Details for the period of Tannenberg's residence at Nazareth are from the diary of the Nazareth congregation, now at the Nazareth Moravian Church. The reference to the washing of the sheep is in the entry for May 14, 1753.

15. Vital statistics for the Tannenberg family are recorded in the Church Register of the Lititz Moravian Church in the archives of that church. There is, however, some question as to whether Anna Maria was born at Nazareth or at Bethlehem.

16. Klemm's memoir is in the Archives of the Moravian Church at Bethlehem. Details of his life are taken from the memoir.

17. J. Taylor Hamilton, "A History of the Church Known as the Moravian Church" in *Transactions of the Moravian Historical Society*, VI, 41. See also Levering, *op. cit.*, p. 171.

18. Samuel Kriebel Brecht, *The Genealogical Record of the Schwenkfelder Families* (New York: Rand McNally Co., 1923), pp. 34-35; "Narrative of the Journey of the Schwenkfelders to Pennsylvania, 1733" in *The Pennsylvania Magazine of History and Biography*, X (1886), 167-79; Ralph B. Strassburger and William J. Hinke, *Pennsylvania German Pioneers*, I (Norristown, Pa.: Pennsylvania German Society, 1934), 121-26; Andrew S. Berky (ed.), *The Journals and Papers of David Schultze*, I (Pennsburg, Pa.: The Schwenkfelder Library, 1952), 28-29.

19. Morgan Dix (ed.), *A History of the Parish of Trinity Church in the City of New York*, Part I (New York: G. P. Putnam's Sons, 1898), p. 301. See also A. H. Messiter, *A History of the Choir and Music of Trinity Church, New York* (New York: Edwin S. Gorham, 1906), pp. 290-92.

20. William Berrian, *An Historical Sketch of Trinity Church, New York* (New York: Stanford and Swords, 1847), p. 56.

21. Dix, *op. cit.*, p. 224.

22. *Historical Discourse at the Sesqui-Centennial of Christ Evangelical Lutheran Church on the Tulpehocken near Stouchsburg, Berks County, Pennsylvania* (Lebanon, Pa.: F. J. F. Schantz, 1894), pp. 13, 19. This record indicates that Klemm was working in Philadelphia at this time, which does not agree with his memoir which says that he went to New York in 1745 or 1746.

23. Ernest T. Kretschmann, *The Old Trappe Church* (Philadelphia: Published by the Congregation, 1893), p. 61; and Theodore E. Schmauk, *The Church Organ*

and Its History (unpublished manuscript in the Archives of the Ministerium of Pennsylvania at the Lutheran Theological Seminary in Philadelphia), p. 256.

24. The question has been raised as to whether Klemm was the builder of this first Bethlehem organ, since the records indicate that Gustavus Hesselius actually contracted for the work. This Swedish portrait painter and spinet maker, and sometime Moravian, is also referred to as an organ builder. It seems likely that Klemm, who is referred to here as "the organmaker," was the one who built the instrument, perhaps while he was in the employ of Hesselius. See *Church Music and Musical Life in Pennsylvania in the Eighteenth Century*, II (Philadelphia: Pennsylvania Society of the Colonial Dames of America, 1927), 175, 271; and Donald M. McCorkle, "Prelude to a History of American Moravian Organs" in *American Guild of Organists Quarterly*, Vol. III, No. 4 (October, 1958), pp. 142-43.

25. Franklin, *op. cit.*, p. 236.

26. Diary of the Bethlehem Moravian Congregation, August 20 and September 3, 1751. Other information concerning Hartaffel is in the Burial Book of the Lancaster Moravian Church (in the Bethlehem Archives), and the Church Council Records of the Lancaster Moravian Church, June 6, 1762 (also in the Bethlehem Archives). See also Strassburger and Hinke, *op. cit.*, pp. 359-61; and Franklin Ellis and Samuel Evans, *History of Lancaster County, Pennsylvania* (Philadelphia: Everts and Peck, 1883), pp. 369-70.

27. Information on the stay in Nazareth is from the diary of the Nazareth Moravian Congregation, now at the Nazareth Moravian Church.

28. Diary of the Christian's Spring Moravian Congregation (now at the Nazareth Moravian Church), July, 1760, and memorabilia, 1760. See also James Henry, "Christian's Spring" in *Transactions of the Moravian Historical Society*, Vol. I, No. 2 (1857-58), p. 75.

29. Bethlehem Moravian Elders' Conference, December 9, 1762.

30. Diary of the Bethlehem Moravian Congregation, August 19, 1762.

31. Bethlehem Moravian Elders' Conference, July 5, 1762.

32. The copy consulted is in the Archives of the Moravian Music Foundation, Winston-Salem, North Carolina.

33. Charles W. McManis and Frank P. Albright, "Tannenberg Restoration" in *The Tracker*, Vol. IX, No. 2 (Winter, 1965), p. 2.

34. Rudyard Kipling, *Rewards and Fairies* (London: Macmillan and Co., Ltd., 1914), p. 138.

35. John G. Zook, *Historical and Pictorial Lititz* (Lititz, Pa.: Express Printing Co., 1905), pp. 202-3.

36. Diaries of the Bethlehem and Lititz Moravian Congregations for November, 1761.

37. Diary of the Lancaster Moravian Congregation, April 20 to May 6, 1765. Also Lancaster Moravian Church Council Records, September 12, 1762.

38. The property is described in the records of the U. S. Direct Tax of 1798, in the National Archives, Washington, D. C.

39. Letter from Tannenberg to Nathaniel Seidel, June 30, 1766.

40. Herbert H. Beck, *op. cit.*, pp. 105-20.

41. *Ibid.*, p. 115.

42. Bethlehem Moravian Elders' Conference, November 19, 1781.

43. Paul E. Beck, "David Tanneberger, Organ Builder" in *Papers Read Before the Lancaster County Historical Society,* Vol. XXX, No. 1 (1926), p. 10.

44. Thomas Anburey, *Travels Through the Interior Parts of America,* II (Boston and New York: Houghton Mifflin Co., 1923), 300.

45. Inventory of Lititz Church and Congregation House, 1765.

46. See Donald M. McCorkle, "The Moravian Contribution to American Music" in *Music Library Association Notes,* Vol. XIII, No. 4 (September, 1956), pp. 597-99; and Joseph A. Maurer, "The Moravian Trombone Choir" in *Historical Review of Berks County,* Vol. XX, No. 1 (October-December, 1954), pp. 2-8.

47. Herbert H. Beck, "Lititz as an Early Musical Center" in *Papers Read Before the Lancaster County Historical Society,* Vol. XIX, No. 3 (1915), p. 73. See also Theo. M. Finney, "The Collegium Musicum at Lititz, Pennsylvania, During the Eighteenth Century" in *Papers Read by Members of the American Musicological Society* (1937).

48. Kipling, *op. cit.,* "Brother Square Toes" and "A Priest in Spite of Himself." Hirte himself wrote at least two books: *Ein neues, auserlesenes, gemeinnütziges Hand-Büchlein* (Chestnut Hill, Pa.: Samuel Saur, 1792) and *Der Freund in der Noth, oder Zweyter Theil, des Neuen, Auserlesenen Gemeinnützigen Hand-Büchlein* (Germantaun, Pa.: Peter Leibert, 1793).

49. Diary of the Lititz Moravian Single Brethren's Choir, May 28-30, 1791.

50. Donald M. McCorkle, *Moravian Music in Salem: A German-American Heritage* (Ann Arbor, Mich.: University Microfilms, Inc., 1958), pp. 55, 161. See also Finney, *op. cit., passim.*

51. Finney, *op. cit.,* p. 49.

52. Diary of the Lititz Moravian Single Brethren's Choir, August 29, 1771. The two are listed as *cantores* and *violisten* on a loose memorandum in the archives of the Lititz Moravian Church, dated July, 1779.

53. Lititz Moravian Aufseher Collegium, September 27, 1793.

54. Lititz Moravian Elders' Conference, January 13, 1800.

55. Letter from Tannenberg to Ferdinand Detmers, August 25, 1790, now in the archives of the Lititz Moravian Church.

56. *German-American Annals,* VI, 256, quoted in Carl Wittke, *We Who Built America: The Saga of the Immigrant* (Cleveland: The Press of Western Reserve University, 1939), p. 71.

57. H. L. Mencken, *The American Language,* Supplement I (New York: Alfred A. Knopf, 1962), pp. 138-40.

58. Diary of the Philadelphia Moravian Congregation, October 22-29, 1766.

59. Diary of the Lititz Moravian Congregation, September 14 and November 6, 1767. Diary of the New York Moravian Congregation, September-October, 1767.

60. Diary of the Lititz Moravian Congregation, August 15 and November 22, 1768.

61. Diary of the Lititz Moravian Congregation, June 15 and October 21, 1769. Diary of the Philadelphia Moravian Congregation, October 5 and 19, 1769.

62. Diary of the Lititz Moravian Congregation, September 5, 1767. See also the copy of the diary now at the Lititz Church for this date.

63. Diary of the Lititz Moravian Congregation, November 17, 1768.

64. *Pennsylvania Gazette,* January 10, 1771, quoted in Paul E. Beck, *op. cit.,* p. 5. A similar report appeared in *Der Wöchentliche Pennsylvanische Staatsbote* of Heinrich Miller, No. 482, April 16, 1771.

65. Burial Book of St. Michael's and Zion Lutheran Churches, Philadelphia, Pennsylvania.

66. *Pennsylvania Gazette,* December 30, 1762, quoted in R. R. Drummond, *Early German Music in Philadelphia* (New York: D. Appleton and Co., 1910), p. 22.

67. These two men visited his shop in 1762 to inspect a clavichord which Stiegel was having built. See George L. Heiges, *Henry William Stiegel and His Associates* (Lancaster, Pa.: Rudisill and Co., Inc., 1948) pp. 69-70.

68. Contract with Feyring is in the archives of First Reformed Church (United Church of Christ), Philadelphia. Other information from records copied by William J. Hinke in the Archives of the Historical Society of the Evangelical and Reformed Church, Lancaster, Pennsylvania.

69. Benjamin Dorr, *A Historical Account of Christ Church, Philadelphia* (Philadelphia: R. S. H. George, 1841), pp. 145, 158-59, 325; Drummond, *op. cit.,* pp. 21-22; Eugene M. McCracken, "Duck Soup" in *The Tracker,* Vol. IV, No. 1 (October, 1959), pp. 9-12.

70. *Pennsylvania Gazette,* December 30, 1762, quoted in Drummond, *op. cit.,* pp. 21-22.

71. Lititz Moravian Elders' Conference, November 12, 1770.

72. Diary of the Lititz Moravian Congregation, November 21 (23?), 1771.

73. Diary of the Lititz Moravian Congregation, May 29 and June 6, 1775 (copy at the Lititz Church).

74. Jacob Fry, *The History of Trinity Lutheran Church, Reading, Pennsylvania* (Reading: Published by the Congregation, 1894), pp. 90-91.

75. Thomas Anburey, *op. cit.,* II, 176-77.

76. Lititz Moravian Elders' Conference, August 5, 1776; Diary of the Lititz Moravian Single Sisters' Choir, August 5, 1776, and November 15, 1777. Diary of the Lititz Moravian Congregation, August 4-5, 1776.

77. Abraham R. Beck, "Extracts from the Brethren's House and Congregational Diaries of the Moravian Church at Lititz, Pennsylvania, Relating to the Revolutionary War" in *The Penn Germania,* Vol. I, Nos. 11-12 (November-December, 1912), p. 849.

78. Cited in Schmauk, *op. cit.,* p. 277. The origin of the organ in the Single Sisters' House is not known, but it may well have been an additional work of Tannenberg or Klemm.

79. Abraham R. Beck, *op. cit.,* p. 849.

80. *Loc. cit.*

81. *Ibid.,* p. 852. For this incident, see also the Diary of the Lititz Moravian Congregation, October 21, 1777, and Diary of the Lititz Moravian Single Brethren's Choir, October 21-23, 1777.

82. Abraham R. Beck, *op. cit.,* p. 853.

83. Details of the Lititz hospital are from Abraham R. Beck, *op. cit.,* pp. 854-58, and two articles by Herbert H. Beck, "Graveyard of the Revolutionary Soldiers at Lititz" and "The Military Hospital at Lititz, 1777-78" both in *Historical Papers and Addresses of the Lancaster County Historical Society,* the former in Vol. XXXVII (1933), pp. 1-5, and the latter in Vol. XXIII, No. 1, pp. 5-14.

84. Lititz Moravian Elders' Conference, January 19, 1778.

85. George Blumer, "Dr. William Brown" in *Dictionary of American Biography,* III (New York: Charles Scribner's Sons, 1929), 157. See also Bessie W. Gahn, "Dr. William Brown, Physician-General to the American Army" in *Journal of the American Pharmaceutical Association,* Vol. XVI, No. 11 (November, 1927), pp. 1090-91.

86. Abraham R. Beck, *op. cit.,* p. 859.

87. William Brown, *Pharmacopoeia Simpliciorum et Efficaciorum* . . . (Philadelphia: Styner and Cist, 1778).

88. Letter from Matthew Hehl to William Shippen, April 9, 1778, and reply of the same date.

89. Kenneth Gardiner Hamilton, *John Ettwein and the Moravian Church During the Revolutionary Period* (Bethlehem, Pa.: Times Publishing Co., 1940), pp. 132-38, 211; and "A Petition by the Moravians During the American Revolution" in *The Pennsylvania German,* Vol. XII, No. 1 (1911), pp. 43-45. For the effect of the Test Act on the Lititz congregation, see Abraham R. Beck, *op. cit.,* pp. 857-59.

90. Lititz Moravian Elders' Conference, April 28-December 1, 1781; and Thomas Lynch Montgomery (ed.), *Pennsylvania Archives,* Fifth Series, VII, 237, 274, 281, 283, 329.

91. Letter from Bernhard Adam Grube to Nathaniel Seidel, October 3, 1765.

92. Lititz Moravian Aufseher Collegium, November 8, 1772.

93. Letter from John Gottfried Zahm to Nathaniel Seidel, September 7, 1780.

94. Lititz Moravian Elders' Conference, October 30, 1779.

95. *Ibid.,* August 27, 1770.

96. Lititz Moravian Aufseher Collegium, June 21, 1781.

97. The will is in Lancaster County, Pennsylvania, Will Book H, Vol. I, p. 540.

98. Letter from Bernhard Adam Grube to Nathaniel Seidel, January 16, 1778.

99. Diary of the York Moravian Congregation, August 17 to September 7, 1784.

100. Lititz Moravian Aufseher Collegium, January 14, 1786.

101. John W. Lippold, "Old Trinity Steeple" in *Historical Papers and Addresses of the Lancaster County Historical Society,* Vol. XXXI, No. 9 (1927), p. 129.

102. Paul E. Beck, *op. cit.,* p. 11.

103. The Lancaster trip is recorded in the Diary of the Lancaster Moravian Congregation, November 1-10, 1784. The Philadelphia-Bethlehem trip is in the Diary of the Lititz Moravian Congregation, October 11, 1785.

104. Lititz Moravian Elders' Conference, May 18 and 25, 1782.

105. Lititz Moravian Aufseher Collegium, December 28, 1780.

106. Tannenberg's will in Lancaster County, Pennsylvania, Will Book H, Vol. I, p. 540.

107. *Neue Unpartheyische Lancäster Zeitung,* June 25, 1788.

108. Diary of the Lititz Moravian Congregation, report (*Bericht*) for May and June, 1788; see also the Diary of the Lititz Moravian Single Brethren's Choir, June 17, 1788.

119. *Neue Unpartheyische Lancäster Zeitung,* June 25, 1788.

110. C. R. Demme, *Zum Andenken an die Hundertjährige Jubelfeier in der deutschen evangel. luther. St. Michaelis-Kirche in Philadelphia* (Philadelphia: Conrad Zentler, 1843), p. 79.

111. Letter from Tannenberg to Ferdinand Detmers, August 25, 1790, now in the archives of the Lititz Moravian Church.

112. See the diary of Justus Henry Christian Helmuth, July through October, 1790.

113. *Neue Philadelphische Correspondez*, No. 4, October 12, 1790. See also the printed program of the service, *Lob und Anbetung des Gottmenschen, am Tage der Einweihung der neuen Orgel in der Deutschen Evangelisch Lutherischen Zions Kirche in Philadelphia, den 10 October, 1790* (Germantaun, Pa.: Michael Billmeyer, 1790).

114. Letter from Tannenberg to Ferdinand Detmers, September 21, 1790, now in the archives of the Lititz Moravian Church.

115. *Ibid.*

116. *Ibid.* Details of the fire are from Helmuth's Diary for December 26, 1794; W. J. Mann and A. Spaeth, *Fest-Gruss zum Zions-Jubiläum, Mai 13, 1866* (Philadelphia: C. W. Widmaier, 1866), p. 30; and Jacob Cox Parsons (ed.), *Extracts from the Diary of Jacob Hiltzheimer of Philadelphia, 1765-98* (Philadelphia: William F. Fell and Co., 1893), p. 210. See also *The Philadelphia Gazette*, January 1 and 7, 1795, and *The Philadelphia General Advertiser (Aurora)*, December 27, 1794.

117. Memoir of Anna Rosina Kern Tannenberg in the archives of the Lititz Moravian Church.

118. Death Register of the Philadelphia Moravian Congregation, October 18-20, 1793.

119. Lititz Moravian Elders' Conference, March 3 and August 25, 1803.

120. Marriage Record of First Reformed Church, Philadelphia, August 30, 1797.

121. This raises the question of how the Krauss brothers came to be organ builders. It is possible that some of Klemm's knowledge was available to the Krauss family. In any case, it is known that the Krausses had built at least two organs before their association with David Tannenberg, Jr. But the services of the younger Tannenberg must have taught them much. John Krauss also possessed a copy of a work on organ building by Georg Andreas Sorge, which he had copied November 8, 1798. The younger Tannenberg was then in his employ and the work may well have come from the Tannenbergs. Various Krauss manuscripts, including that of Sorge, are now deposited in the Schwenkfelder Library, Pennsburg, Pennsylvania. For further information on the Krausses, see Samuel K. Brecht, *op. cit.*, pp. 146-59; William U. Kistler, "Early Organ Builders in Northern Montgomery County" in *Historical Sketches of the Historical Society of Montgomery County, Pennsylvania*, IV (1910), 112-17; E. S. Gerhard (ed.), *Schwenkfelder Craftsmen, Inventors, and Surveyors*, Schwenkfeldiana, Vol. I, No. 5 (Norristown, Pa.: Board of Publication of the Schwenkfelder Church, 1945), pp. 12-18, 29-33; and "Ancient Home of Old Organ Builders" in *The Pennsylvania German*, Vol. X, No. 4 (1909), pp. 174-75.

122. Diary of John Krauss, Vol. I, March 29, 1798, to August 2, 1799. The diary is in the Schwenkfelder Library. The Goshenhoppen organ was used later in the Catholic Church in Bally, Berks County. The case of this organ is very similar to those of Tannenberg.

123. Lititz Moravian Elders' Conference, October 28, 1786. See also letter from Johann Andreas Hübner to John Ettwein, April 3, 1791.

124. Letter from Johann Andreas Hübner to John Ettwein, April 3, 1791.

125. Letter from Johann Andreas Hübner to John Ettwein, February 15, 1793. For the marriage, see the Diary of the Lititz Moravian Congregation, April 16, 1793.

126. Diary of the Lititz Moravian Congregation, November 15, 1837 (Bachmann's memoir), in the Archives of the Moravian Church at Bethlehem.

127. James Owen Knauss, Jr., *Social Conditions Among the Pennsylvania Germans in the Eighteenth Century, as Revealed in the German Newspapers Published in America* (Lancaster, Pa.: Vol. XXIX, Publications of the Pennsylvania German Society, 1922), p. 47.

128. Adelaide L. Fries (ed.), *Records of the Moravians in North Carolina,* VI (Raleigh: North Carolina Historical Commission, 1943), 2508-10, 2512, 2539-40, 2567, 2591-92, 2603, 2605.

129. Diary of the Lititz Moravian Congregation, February 6, 1799; Abraham R. Beck, *The Moravian Graveyards of Lititz, Pennsylvania, 1744-1905* (n.d.), pp. 247-48.

130. Letter from Tannenberg to Samuel Stotz, December 7, 1800, now in the archives of the Moravian Music Foundation.

131. She was born Anna Maria Fischer, February 2, 1743, at Heidelberg, Pennsylvania. She was married first in 1772 to James Hall, who died in 1783, and secondly in 1785 to Gottlieb Lange, who died in 1792. She died April 19, 1820. The process of her selection as Tannenberg's wife is recorded in Lititz Moravian Elders' Conference, March through May, 1800. Her memoir is in the archives of the Lititz Moravian Church. See also Abraham R. Beck, *The Moravian Graveyards of Lititz, Pennsylvania, 1744-1905* (n.d.), p. 259, and Lititz Moravian Death Register, April 19, 1820, at the Lititz Moravian Church.

132. Letter from Tannenberg to Samuel Stotz, December 7, 1800, now in the archives of the Moravian Music Foundation.

133. Recorded with the will at the Lancaster County courthouse, Lancaster, Pennsylvania.

134. Letter from Tannenberg to Samuel Stotz, June 11, 1800, now in the archives of the Moravian Music Foundation. Details of Tannenberg's complaints against Bachmann are contained in a series of letters to Salem, all in these archives.

135. Letters from Tannenberg to Bachmann (October 20, 1800) and Samuel Stotz (June 18, 1801) in the archives of the Moravian Music Foundation. This was for the organ built by Joseph Ferdinand Bulitschek in 1773. Tannenberg's price for the pipes was £15. See Donald M. McCorkle, *Moravian Music in Salem: A German-American Heritage* (Ann Arbor, Mich.: University Microfilms, Inc., 1958), pp. 74-76.

136. Letter from Tannenberg to Friederick Marschall, October 17, 1800, in the archives of the Moravian Music Foundation.

137. Letter from Tannenberg to Samuel Stotz, December 7, 1800, in the archives of the Moravian Music Foundation.

138. Lititz Moravian Aufseher Collegium, December 1, 1800.

139. *Ibid.,* November 10-11, 1801; Lititz Moravian Elders' Conference, November 14, 1801.

140. Information from the Bachmann family through Mrs. Harvey Bachman of Lititz, Pennsylvania.

141. Levering, *op. cit.,* p. 364 n. Ernst Julius Bachmann's memoir is in the archives of the Lititz Moravian Church.

142. Johann Philip Bachmann's memoir is contained in the Diary of the Lititz Moravian Congregation, November 15, 1837.

143. Lititz Moravian Elders' Conference, February 14 and 28 and March 9, 1793, and June 18 and 22, 1795; Diary of the Lititz Moravian Congregation, July 11, 1795.

144. Lititz Moravian Elders' Conference, December 14, 1797; July 11, 1799; January 12, 1803.

145. Levering, *op. cit.*, pp. 577-78; Letter from Johannes Herbst to Bethlehem, May 19, 1804.

146. Maria Elisabeth Tannenberg Schropp's memoir and silhouette are in the Archives of the Moravian Church at Bethlehem.

147. *Der Americanische Staatsbote,* May 30, 1804.

148. Details from Tannenberg's memoir.

149. Letter from Tannenberg to John Schropp, April 20, 1804. John Hall, who delivered the letter, was Tannenberg's stepson. Lewis Miller's sketch of Tannenberg in York depicts a "Mr. Hall" who "finishes the organ." This may have been John Hall or another stepson, or it may have been one of the Hall family of organ builders who later appear in Philadelphia and then in New York. (Is it possible that there is some connection between Tannenberg's stepsons and the Halls of Philadelphia?)

150. Diary of the York Moravian Congregation, May 17-21, 1804. Details also from the memoirs of Tannenberg and his wife.

151. Abraham R. Beck, "David Tannenberg" in *The Pennsylvania German,* Vol. X, No. 7 (July, 1909), pp. 339-40. The bodies in the Moravian Cemetery were later removed to Prospect Hill Cemetery on North George Street in York. Tannenberg's grave is located in Section N.

152. From the files of the Historical Society of York County, Pennsylvania. Ludwig Miller was the father of Lewis Miller, who left the only known picture of Tannenberg.

PART II

1. Selections from this and Schweitzer's other works on organs and organ building are given in Charles R. Joy, *Music in the Life of Albert Schweitzer* (Boston: Beacon Paperback, 1951). See also Schweitzer's *Out of My Life and Thought* (New York: Mentor, 1955), especially chapter 8.

2. A concise work is John Broadhouse, *The Organ Viewed from Within* (London: William Reeves, n.d.). See also the bibliography.

3. *Neue Unpartheyische Lancäster Zeitung,* November 19, 1788.

4. Diary of the Lancaster Moravian Congregation, April 30, 1765.

5. Archives of Zion Lutheran Church, Baltimore, Maryland. The subscription list is dated January 5, 1795.

6. Diary of the Graceham Moravian Congregation, May 27, 1792.

7. Letter from Tannenberg to Friederick Marschall, December 11, 1797, now in the archives of the Moravian Music Foundation.

8. Joseph Mortimer Levering, *A History of Bethlehem, Pennsylvania, 1741-1892* (Bethlehem: Times Publishing Co., 1903), pp. 577-78.

9. Adelaide L. Fries (ed.), *Records of the Moravians in North Carolina*, VI (Raleigh: North Carolina Historical Commission, 1943), 2512.

10. Letters from Tannenberg to Bethlehem officials (March 16, 1803) and John Schropp (April 20, 1804).

11. The specifications were altered somewhat when the contract was finally signed. The specifications from the contract are given in full in Part III.

12. The original contract is in the archives of First Reformed Church (United Church of Christ), Lancaster, Pennsylvania.

13. Diary of the Lititz Moravian Congregation, July 30, 1770.

14. *Records and Notes of Interest in Church Affairs, 1758-1825* (V-102), p. 184 (September 2, 1771) in the archives of Trinity Lutheran Church, Lancaster, Pennsylvania.

15. *Pennsylvania Gazette*, December 23, 1762, quoted in R. R. Drummond, *Early German Music in Philadelphia* (New York: D. Appleton and Co., 1910), p. 21.

16. The building measured twenty by fifteen feet (Records of the U. S. Direct Tax of 1798 in the National Archives, Washington, D. C.).

17. Letter from Bernhard Adam Grube to Nathaniel Seidel, January 16, 1778; Lititz Moravian Elders' Conference, February 11, 1771.

18. Minutes of the Lititz Moravian Congregation Council, May 5, 1766.

19. Diary of the Nazareth Moravian Congregation, July 19, 1762.

20. Minutes of the Lititz Moravian Congregation Council, February 14, 1771; Lititz Moravian Elders' Conference, January 14, May 18 and 27, August 16 and 19, 1771, April 5, May 12, and June 21, 1773, and June 13, 1789; Lititz Moravian Aufseher Collegium, June 26, 1773.

21. Donald M. McCorkle, "Prelude to a History of American Moravian Organs" in *American Guild of Organists Quarterly*, Vol. III, No. 4 (October, 1958), pp. 145-46. A native of Bohemia, Bulitschek was born in 1729, came to Bethlehem in 1754 and to Lititz in 1759. See also Diary of the Bethlehem Moravian Single Brethren's Choir, April 24, 1759; Fries, *op. cit.*, Vols. I through VII, *passim;* and John W. Jordan, "Moravian Immigration to Pennsylvania, 1734-67" in *Transactions of the Moravian Historical Society*, Vol. V, No. 2, p. 79.

22. Catalogue of the Congregation in Lititz, June 20, 1784.

23. "Inventory of Instrument Maker" dated July 5, 1762. Copy consulted is in the files of Historic Bethlehem, Inc.

24. *Philadelphia Gazette*, January 7, 1795; William Guthrie, *A New System of Modern Geography*, II (Philadelphia: Printed for Matthew Carey, 1795), 447.

25. "Quantitative spectrochemical analysis of one sample of organ pipe metal" in File 430-5 at the Historical Society of York County; Charles W. McManis and Frank P. Albright, "Tannenberg Restoration" in *The Tracker*, Vol. IX, No. 2 (Winter, 1965), p. 8. Among the Krauss papers in the Schwenkfelder Library there is a "recipe" for making solder to be used on organ pipes. It consists of five parts tin, three parts bismuth, and three parts lead.

26. Letter from Tannenberg to Samuel Stotz, December 7, 1800, now in the archives of the Moravian Music Foundation. For the Bachmann organ, see the Appendix.

27. Paul E. Beck, "David Tanneberger, Organ Builder" in *Papers Read Before the Lancaster County Historical Society*, Vol. XXX, No. 1 (1926), p. 4.

28. Diary of the Bethlehem Moravian Congregation, January 15, 1758; Letter from Tannenberg to John Schropp, September 23, 1794.

29. Lititz Moravian Elders' Conference, March 10 and 17, 1803.

30. Benjamin Franklin, *The Autobiography of Benjamin Franklin* (New Haven: Yale University Press, 1964), p. 217; William Frederic Worner, *Old Lancaster: Tales and Traditions* (Lancaster, Pa.: Published by the author, 1927), p. 101.

31. See, for example, the account in Charles R. Roberts and J. D. Schindel in *History of Egypt Church* (Allentown, Pa.: Papers Read Before the Lehigh County Historical Society, 1908), p. 62.

32. Letter from Friedrich Leinbach to John Schropp, October 1, 1782; Letter from Tannenberg to Samuel Stotz, June 11, 1800, in the archives of the Moravian Music Foundation; Letter from Tannenberg to Nils Tillofsen, September 22, 1793 (copy consulted is in the Library of the Moravian Historical Society, Nazareth, Pennsylvania).

33. Diary of the Bethlehem Single Brethren's Choir, November 17 through December 1, 1776.

34. Records of Zion Lutheran Church, Baltimore, Maryland, December 4, 1795, *et passim;* Records of First Reformed Church (United Church of Christ), Lancaster, Pennsylvania, March 26, 1771.

35. Beck, *op. cit.,* p. 9. Beck gives an extended description of Tannenberg's bellows on page 10, including an alternate type used for the New Holland organ and others. The Lititz bellows were destroyed in a fire in 1957 (see *The Tracker,* Vol. II, No. 1 [October, 1957], p. 6).

36. Letter from Tannenberg to Nils Tillofsen, September 22, 1793 (see note 32 above); Letter from John Youngberg to John Schropp, November 21, 1793.

37. Records of Trinity Lutheran Church, Lancaster, Pennsylvania. Others were paid for additional woodwork and for the painting.

38. Letter from Nils Tillofsen to John Schropp, December 15, 1793.

39. *Two Centuries of Nazareth, 1740-1940* (Nazareth, Pa.: Bi-centennial, Inc., 1940), pp. 79-80; Roberts and Schindel, *op. cit.,* p. 62; Journal of the Single Brethren at Bethlehem, 1772-1780, account dated November 29, 1776.

40. Donald M. McCorkle, *Moravian Music in Salem: A German-American Heritage* (Ann Arbor, Mich.: University Microfilms, Inc., 1958), p. 69; Harold Donaldson Eberlein and Cortland Van Dyke Hubbard, "Music in the Early Federal Era" in *The Pennsylvania Magazine of History and Biography,* LXIX (1945), 121; Jack Green (ed.), *The Diary of Colonel Landon Carter,* I (Charlottesville, Va.: The University Press of Virginia, 1965), 103.

41. H. M. J. Klein and William F. Diller, *The History of St. James' Church (Protestant Episcopal) 1744-1944* (Lancaster, Pa.: Published by the Vestry, 1944), p. 35.

42. Joseph Henry Dubbs, "Formative Influences" in *The College Student,* March, 1908, p. 154.

43. John C. Ogden, *An Excursion into Bethlehem and Nazareth in Pennsylvania in the Year 1799* (Philadelphia: Charles Cist, 1805), p. 42.

44. The paintings of John Valentine Haidt (1700-1782) are recognized today as among the most important early American religious paintings. A booklet prepared for a recent exhibition at the Abby Aldrich Rockefeller Folk Art Collection,

Williamsburg, Virginia (1966; text by Vernon H. Nelson) is the most extensive treatment of his life and work.

45. L. H. Butterfield (ed.), *Adams Family Correspondence,* II (Cambridge, Mass.: Belknap Press of Harvard University Press, 1963), 155. The letter is dated February 7, 1777, and the organ was therefore the Klemm-Tannenberg instrument of 1759.

46. Among the papers of John Krauss in the Schwenkfelder Library is a "recipe" for making "organ builder's white," the paint used on the organ cases, which Krauss had copied in 1804 from a German text.

47. Diary of the Lancaster Moravian Congregation, April 24-29, 1765.

48. McManis and Albright, *op. cit.,* pp. 2, 8.

49. Diary of the Lititz Moravian Single Brethren's Choir, August 13, 1787.

50. Charles F. Dapp, *History of Zion's or Old Organ Church* (Spring City, Pa.: The Inter-Borough Press, 1919), pp. 46-47; Diary of the Hebron Moravian Congregation, November 14, 1773.

51. *Der Deutsche Porcupein,* No. 56, January 23, 1799.

52. *Neue Unpartheyische Lancäster Zeitung,* August 15, 1787.

53. Diary of the Lititz Moravian Congregation, September 21, 1801; Dapp, *op. cit.,* p. 47.

54. Diary of the Hope Moravian Congregation, October 5, 1782.

55. Diary of the Nazareth Moravian Congregation, December 15-16, 1793.

56. Diary of the Graceham Moravian Congregation, May 4, 1793.

57. Fries (ed.), *op. cit.,* VI, 2656, 2947-52.

58. Green (ed.), *op. cit.,* p. 103.

59. Joy, *op. cit.,* pp. 166-67.

60. Letters from Tannenberg to Samuel Stotz, December 7, 1800, and June 18, 1801, in the archives of the Moravian Music Foundation.

61. The directions are included with a letter from Tannenberg to Samuel Stotz, May 25, 1802, in the archives of the Moravian Music Foundation.

PART III

1. Will Book H, Vol. I, p. 540, at the Lancaster County courthouse, Lancaster, Pennsylvania.

2. This sheet is included with a copy of Tannenberg's memoir in the archives of the Lititz Moravian Church.

3. Paul E. Beck, "David Tanneberger, Organ Builder" in *Papers Read Before the Lancaster County Historical Society,* Vol. XXX, No. 1 (1926), pp. 3-11.

4. Several corrections have been made in Beck's list. The 1761 organ installed by Tannenberg in the Lititz Moravian Chapel was not his work, but the old 1746 Bethlehem organ. The organ for the Single Sisters' House in Lititz was made in 1798 rather than in 1761. And the 1775 organ for Frederick, Maryland, was for the Lutheran rather than the Reformed Church. Some other minor corrections of dates have also been made.

5. Charles R. Joy, *Music in the Life of Albert Schweitzer: With Selections from His Writings* (Boston: Beacon Paperback, 1959), p. 153.

6. Diary of the Nazareth Moravian Congregation, March 1, August 26, and memorabilia, 1758. The diary is in the archives of the Nazareth Moravian Church.

7. Preston A. Barba, *They Came to Emmaus: A History* (Emmaus, Pa.: Published by the Borough of Emmaus, 1959), p. 143.

8. Diary of the Nazareth Moravian Congregation, March 1, December 24, and memorabilia, 1758, in the archives of the Nazareth Moravian Church.

9. Diary of the Bethlehem Moravian Congregation, January 29, 1759.

10. John C. Ogden, *An Excursion into Bethlehem and Nazareth in Pennsylvania in the Year 1799* (Philadelphia: Charles Cist, 1805), p. 34.

11. Joseph Mortimer Levering, *A History of Bethlehem, Pennsylvania, 1741-1892* (Bethlehem: Times Publishing Co., 1903), p. 578.

12. Diary of the Christian's Spring Moravian Congregation, July 1, 10 and memorabilia, 1760. The diary is in the archives of the Nazareth Moravian Church.

13. Diary of the Bethlehem Moravian Congregation, April 20, 1762.

14. Adelaide L. Fries (ed.), *Records of the Moravians in North Carolina,* I (Raleigh: North Carolina Historical Commission, 1922), 247.

15. *Ibid.,* I, 254; II, 835-36.

16. Donald M. McCorkle, *Moravian Music in Salem: A German-American Heritage* (Ann Arbor, Mich.: University Microfilms, Inc., 1958), p. 73.

17. Diary of the Lancaster Moravian Congregation, April 20 through May 6, 1765; Lancaster Moravian Church Council Records, July 7, 1765.

18. S. C. Albright, *The Story of the Moravian Congregation at York, Pennsylvania* (York: The Maple Press Co., foreword dated 1927), pp. 65-66, 138.

19. Diary of the Philadelphia Moravian Congregation, October 29, 1766.

20. Diary of the Lititz Moravian Congregation, September 14 and November 6, 1767.

21. Joel Munsell, *The Annals of Albany,* second edition, I (Albany: Joel Munsell, 1869), 166-67.

22. Diary of the Lititz Moravian Congregation, November 22, 1768.

23. Beck, *op. cit.,* p. 4.

24. Joseph Henry Dubbs, "Formative Influences" in *The College Student,* March, 1908, p. 155.

25. Diary of the Lititz Moravian Congregation, October 21, 1769.

26. Abraham R. Beck, "David Tannenberg" in *The Pennsylvania German,* Vol. X, No. 7 (July, 1909), p. 340.

27. Paul E. Beck, *op. cit.,* p. 4.

28. J. D. Wanner, *Kirchen-Recht der Zions Kirche zu Richmond, Berks County, Pennsylvania* (Kutztown, Pa.: "Geist der Zeit" Druckerei, 1863), p. 15.

29. S. H. Fegely, in *Reading Daily Times* (about 1878). Clipping in the archives of the Historical Society of the Evangelical and Reformed Church, Lancaster, Pennsylvania.

30. *Two Hundredth Anniversary of the Congregation* [Zion-Moselem], *1734-1934,* pages not numbered.

31. Edmund R. Eschbach, *Historic Sketch of the Evangelical Reformed Church of Frederick, Maryland* (1894), pp. 20-21, 39; James B. Ranck, *et al., A History of the Evangelical Reformed Church, Frederick, Maryland* (1964), p. 51.

32. *Kirchen-Buch* (#16698) now in the Hall of Records, Annapolis, Maryland.

33. *Pennsylvania Gazette,* January 10, 1771, quoted in Paul E. Beck, *op. cit.,* p. 5.

34. W. Stuart Cramer, *History of the First Reformed Church, Lancaster, Pennsylvania, 1736-1904*, I (Lancaster: Wickersham Printing Co., 1904), 120.

35. Jacob Fry, *The History of Trinity Lutheran Church, Reading, Pennsylvania* (Reading: Published by the Congregation, 1894), p. 45 *et passim*.

36. Letter from the Secretary, Tinicum United Church of Christ, January, 1966.

37. Diary of the Lititz Moravian Congregation, July 31, 1772. The copy of the diary at the Lititz Moravian Church does not mention the organ but simply notes that the visitors examined the organ shop "with satisfaction."

38. Diary of the Lititz Moravian Congregation, September 3, 1773. From the copy at the Lititz Moravian Church.

39. Diary of the Hebron Moravian Congregation, September through November, 1773.

40. Theodore E. Schmauk, *The Church Organ and Its History* (unpublished manuscript in the Archives of the Ministerium of Pennsylvania at the Lutheran Theological Seminary in Philadelphia), pp. 267-68; William Henry Egle, *History of the County of Lebanon* (Philadelphia: Everts and Peck, 1883), pp. 158-59.

41. *Bi-Centennial, The Moravian Church, Lebanon, Pennsylvania* (1947), p. 28.

42. *Records and Notes of Interest in Church Affairs, 1758-1825* (V-102), p. 184 (September 2, 1771) in the archives of Trinity Lutheran Church, Lancaster, Pennsylvania.

43. Diary of the Lititz Moravian Congregation, December 26, 1774. See also the copy of the diary at the Lititz Moravian Church.

44. C. F. Schaeffer and F. A. Muhlenberg, *Memorial Volume of the Evangelical Lutheran Church of the Holy Trinity, Lancaster, Pennsylvania* (Lancaster: John Baer's Sons, 1861), p. 132.

45. Paul E. Beck, *op. cit.*, p. 5; S. M. Sener, *The Catholic Church at Lancaster, Pennsylvania* (Philadelphia: American Catholic Historical Society, 1894), pp. 18, 21.

46. Abdel Ross Wentz, *History of the Evangelical Lutheran Church of Frederick, Maryland, 1738-1938* (Harrisburg, Pa.: The Evangelical Press, 1938), pp. 143-44.

47. Diary of the Graceham Moravian Congregation, November 25-26, 1775.

48. Wentz, *op. cit.*, pp. 236-37.

49. Diary of the Lititz Moravian Congregation, September 9, 1776.

50. Henry Martyn Kieffer, *Some of the First Settlers of "The Forks of the Delaware" and Their Descendents* (Easton, Pa., 1902), p. 45.

51. *Journals of the House of Representatives of the Commonwealth of Pennsylvania, November 28, 1776-October 2, 1781*, I (Philadelphia: John Dunlap, 1782), 117-22.

52. The stop list and later history of the organ are contained in a memorandum which had been attached to the organ at the Plainfield Church (and is still glued to a board from the organ). The memorandum is now in the possession of the First Reformed Church (United Church of Christ) in Easton. For the later history of the organ, see also W. H. Brong, "History of the Plainfield Church" in *The Pennsylvania German*, Vol. X, No. 7 (July, 1909), p. 371.

53. Diary of the Bethlehem Single Brethren's Choir, November 17 through December 1, 1776; Journal of the Single Brethren at Bethlehem (1772-1780), November 25 through December 17, 1776. The origin of the Brethren's old chapel organ is not known.

54. Paul E. Beck, *op. cit.,* p. 5.

55. Diary of the Lititz Moravian Single Brethren's Choir, January 20, 1768.

56. Diary of the Lititz Moravian Single Brethren's Choir, August 29 and memorabilia, 1777; Diary of the Lititz Moravian Congregation, August 30, 1777.

57. Newton D. Mereness, *Travels in the American Colonies* (New York: Antiquarian Press, Ltd., 1961), p. 612.

58. George R. Prowell, *History of York County, Pennsylvania,* II (Chicago: J. H. Beers and Co., 1907), 111; George H. Eckhardt, *Pennsylvania Clocks and Clockmakers* (New York: Devin-Adair Co., 1955), p. 211.

59. Diary of the Hope Moravian Congregation, October through December and memorabilia, 1782; Hope Moravian Church Council Minutes, October 5, 1782.

60. Diary of the Lititz Moravian Congregation, June 21, 1783.

61. Diary of the Lititz Moravian Congregation, August 17, 1784; Diary of the York Moravian Congregation, August 17 through September 7, 1784.

62. John C. Fitzpatrick (ed.), *The Diaries of George Washington,* IV (Boston and New York: Houghton Mifflin Co., 1925), 203.

63. John Gibson (ed.), *History of York County, Pennsylvania* (Chicago: F. A. Battey Publishing Co., 1886), pp. 530-32.

64. Charles R. Roberts and J. D. Schindel, *History of Egypt Church* (Allentown, Pa.: Papers Read Before the Lehigh County Historical Society, 1908), pp. 18-24 *et passim.*

65. Lititz Moravian Aufseher Collegium, January through May, 1786.

66. Lititz Moravian Elders' Conference, May 22, 1786.

67. Letter from Tannenberg to Friedrich Marschall, December 11, 1797, now in the archives of the Moravian Music Foundation.

68. *Neue Unpartheyische Lancäster Zeitung,* August 15, 1787.

69. Paul E. Beck, *op. cit.,* pp. 5-6.

70. *Philadelphia Gazette,* January 7, 1795; *Philadelphische Correspondenz,* No. 370, January 13, 1795.

71. Edward C. Wolf, "The Tannenberg Organ at Old Zion Church, Philadelphia" in *Journal of Church Music,* Vol. III, No. 4 (April, 1961), pp. 2-5; W. J. Mann and A. Spaeth, *Fest-Gruss zum Zions-Jubiläum, Mai 13, 1866* (Philadelphia: C. W. Widmaier, 1866), p. 30.

72. *Lob und Anbetung des Gottmenschen* . . . (Germantaun, Pa.: Michael Billmeyer, 1790).

73. Eugene E. McCracken, "Pennsylvania, the Keystone State" in *The Tracker,* Vol. IV, No. 2 (January, 1960), p. 3.

74. Wolf, *op. cit.,* p. 5.

75. Diary of the Lititz Moravian Congregation, May 12, 1795.

76. Charles F. Dapp, *History of Zion's or Old Organ Church* (Spring City, Pa.: The Inter-Borough Press, 1919), pp. 45-50.

77. Diary of the Graceham Moravian Congregation, May 27, 1792, April 25 through May 5, 1793; see also A. L. Oerter, "Graceham, Frederick County, Maryland, An Historical Sketch" in *Transactions of the Moravian Historical Society,* Vol. IX Nos. 3-4 (1913), pp. 161-62, 203.

78. Diary of the Nazareth Moravian Single Brethren's Choir, November 12, 1793; Diary of the Nazareth Moravian Congregation, November 14 through December 16, 1793; Nazareth Moravian Aufseher Collegium, July, 1792, through

December, 1793. Originals are at the Nazareth Moravian Church. Translations consulted are in the Library of the Moravian Historical Society at Nazareth.

79. Specifications are from a memorandum sent from Nazareth to Salem, North Carolina, January 16, 1798, and now in the archives of the Moravian Music Foundation.

80. Abraham Ritter, *History of the Moravian Church in Philadelphia, From Its Foundation in 1742 to the Present Time* (Philadelphia: Hayes and Zell, 1857), pp. 59 n. and 261.

81. Minutes of the Board of Corporation, First Reformed Church, August 26, 1790, and August 19, 1836, in the archives of First Reformed Church (United Church of Christ), Philadelphia.

82. Letter from J. A. Hübner to John Ettwein, August 12, 1795. It is possible that "Guts'town" refers to Kutztown, Pennsylvania, but no records of an organ from this period have been found in that locality.

83. W. J. Kershner and Adam G. Lerch, *History of St. John's (Hain's) Reformed Church in Lower Heidelberg Township, Berks County, Pennsylvania* (Reading, Pa.: I. M. Beaver, 1916), pp. 58, 477-78.

84. Records at Zion Lutheran Church, Baltimore (in Record Books #2-4); see also Klaus G. Wust, *Zion in Baltimore, 1755-1955* (Baltimore: Zion Church of the City of Baltimore, 1955), pp. 36, 41-44, 73.

85. Diary of the Lititz Moravian Congregation, October 17, 1797.

86. *Two Hundredth Anniversary, First Ziegel Church, 1750-1950*, p. 4.

87. Account sheet with Tannenberg's memoir at the Lititz Moravian Church lists an organ for "Maccungie." See also note 85 above.

88. Alfred Matthews and Austin N. Hungerford, *History of the Counties of Lehigh and Carbon* (Philadelphia: Everts and Richards, 1884), p. 466.

89. Diary of John Krauss at the Schwenkfelder Library, Pennsburg, Pennsylvania.

90. Original contract is at the Schwenkfelder Library. Photograph is at St. Peter's United Church of Christ.

91. Charles W. McManis and Frank P. Albright, "Tannenberg Restoration" in *The Tracker*, Vol. IX, No. 2 (Winter, 1965); Charles W. McManis, "Restoration of Tannenberg Organ at Old Salem" in *The Diapason*, Vol. 56, No. 4 (March, 1965), pp. 36-37; Charles W. McManis, "David Tannenberg and the Old Salem Restoration" in *The American Organist*, Vol. 48, No. 5 (May, 1965), pp. 15-20.

92. Diary of the Lititz Moravian Single Sisters' Choir, July 10-11 and 26, 1798; Diary of the Lititz Moravian Congregation, July 26 *(Bericht)*, 1798.

93. Diary of the Lancaster Moravian Congregation, January 14, 1798.

94. *Ibid.*, January 17-21, 1799.

95. *Kirchen-Buch* at St. John's Church, pp. 282-83.

96. Clara A. Beck, "St. John's Lutheran Church, Centre Square" in *Historical Sketches of the Historical Society of Montgomery County, Pennsylvania*, V, 67-68; *Record Book, 1865-1909*, for January 7, 1889, at St. John's Church.

97. Letters from Tannenberg to Salem officials, October 17, 1800; December 7, 1800; June 18, 1801; and May 25, 1802; all in the archives of the Moravian Music Foundation. See also Fries (ed.), *op. cit.*, VI, 2655.

98. Fries (ed), *op. cit.*, VI, 2610-11, 2627, 2639, 2947-52.

99. Paul E. Beck, *op. cit.*, pp. 8-9; Charles W. McManis, "David Tannenberg

and the Old Salem Restoration" in *The American Organist,* Vol. 48, No. 5 (May, 1965), pp. 16-17; Charles W. McManis, "Restoration of Tannenberg Organ at Old Salem" in *The Diapason,* Vol. 56, No. 4 (March, 1965), p. 36.

100. [C. G. Bachman], *St. Stephen Reformed Church, New Holland, Pennsylvania* (1951), p. 24.

101. D. W. Gerhard, *A History of the New Holland Charge of the Reformed Church in Lancaster County, Pennsylvania* (New Holland, 1877), p. 62.

102. Paul E. Beck, *op. cit.,* p. 9.

103. W. P. Huddle, *History of the Hebron Lutheran Church, Madison County, Virginia, from 1717 to 1907* (New Market, Va.: Henkel and Co., 1908), pp. 49-51.

104. Schoeneck Moravian Church Council Records, October 10, 1802.

105. Charles W. McManis, "David Tannenberg and the Old Salem Restoration" in *The American Organist,* Vol. 48, No. 5 (May, 1965), p. 17.

106. See above, Part I, Chapter 8.

107. Quoted in the October 6, 1960, concert program at the Historical Society of York County. See also Biggs' article "Welcome Back American Trackers" in *The Diapason,* Vol. 51, No. 10 (September 1, 1960), pp. 18-19.

108. "Tannenberg Organ Restored" in *The American Organist,* Vol. 43, No. 5 (May, 1960), p. 28. The work of restoration is described in Thomas S. Eader, "David Tannenberg's Last Organ" in *The Tracker,* Vol. IV, No. 3 (April, 1960), pp. 3-4. See also "Organ of 1804 Restored" in *The Diapason,* Vol. 51, No. 4 (March 1, 1960), p. 6.

109. Original contract between Tannenberg and the Bethlehem congregation, July 25, 1803, now in the Archives of the Moravian Church at Bethlehem.

110. Diary of the Nazareth Moravian Congregation, January 29, 1759, at the Nazareth Moravian Church.

111. Diary of the Bethlehem Moravian Congregation, November 17, 1761.

112. McCorkle, *op. cit.,* p. 71.

113. Fries (ed.), *op. cit.,* V, 2268.

114. Letter from Tannenberg to Samuel Stotz, November 13, 1799, in the archives of the Moravian Music Foundation.

115. Account sheet with Tannenberg's memoir in the archives of the Lititz Moravian Church. The piano for Brother Lembke was made between 1795 and 1799; the one for the *Kinder-Haus* between 1799 and the time of Tannenberg's death.

APPENDIX

1. Theodore E. Schmauk, *The Church Organ and Its History* (unpublished manuscript in the Archives of the Ministerium of Pennsylvania at the Lutheran Theological Seminary in Philadelphia), pp. 275-76; Schoeneck Moravian Church Council, July 4, 1802, through February 20, 1803; Schoeneck Moravian Congregation Diary, January, 1803.

2. Ellis S. Hay, *One Hundred and Forty-Four Years: A Sketch of Emmanuel Reformed Church, Hanover, Pennsylvania, 1765-1909,* pages not numbered. Additional information from Donald Pfaff, the present organist of Emmanuel Church.

3. Theodore E. Schmauk, *Old Salem in Lebanon* (Lebanon, Pa.: Congregation of Salem Evangelical Lutheran Church, 1898), p. 161.

4. William Henry Egle, *History of the County of Lebanon* (Philadelphia: Everts and Peck, 1883), p. 187.

5. Information furnished by Arthur G. Schuman, Reading, Pennsylvania.

6. D. M. Gilbert (ed.), *Centennial of Zion Lutheran Church, Harrisburg* (Harrisburg, Pa.: Herr Publishing Co., 1896), pp. 133, 136.

7. Egle, *op. cit.,* p. 207.

8. "An Organ of 1819: Built by Philip Bachman" in *The American Organist,* Vol. 16, No. 5 (May, 1933), p. 262.

9. Eugene M. McCracken, "The Spirits Cost $0.75" in *The Tracker,* Vol. V, No. 2 (January, 1961), pp. 6-7.

BIBLIOGRAPHY

MANUSCRIPTS

The Moravian Church has traditionally maintained a careful and rich record of its affairs, both spiritual and temporal. In addition to the usual ledgers, letters, and reports, there are several uniquely Moravian types of record. The Church asked each of its members to write a memoir *(Lebens-lauf)* or autobiography which, after the individual's death, was amplified by the clergy or family, read at the subject's funeral service, and circulated among the other congregations. These often contain quite valuable biographical information and provide an insight into the religious experience of the Moravians.

There was also in each Moravian community a diarist who recorded the daily events of the community and its members. Especially in the earlier years these provide many graphic details of Moravian life. The individual choirs, in some cases, also kept diaries which detail the life of the choir and add perspective and detail to the life of the community. The minutes of the Church Council, the Elders' Conference, the Helpers' Conference, and the *Aufseher Collegium* (Committee on Oversight) are further valuable sources.

Most of the Moravian records consulted are in the Archives of the Moravian Church in Bethlehem, Pennsylvania. Other valuable records are in the archives of the Moravian Church in Lititz, Pennsylvania, including a copy of the diary of the Lititz congregation which is similar to but not identical with the copy at Bethlehem. References to Moravian materials, including documents concerning Lititz, can be assumed to be in the Bethlehem Archives unless otherwise noted. Most of the Moravian manuscripts relating to music have been collected in the archives of the Moravian Music Foundation in Winston-Salem, North Carolina. Included among these are a number of letters and drawings sent by Tannenberg to the Moravians in North Carolina.

Materials relating to the Schwenkfelders are in the Schwenkfelder Library, Pennsburg, Pennsylvania. Records of the German Reformed Churches are in the archives of the Historical Society of the Evangelical and

135

Reformed Church, Fackenthal Library, Franklin and Marshall College,
Lancaster, Pennsylvania. Records of the Lutheran Churches are in the
Archives of the Ministerium of Pennsylvania, located in the Library of the
Lutheran Theological Seminary, Philadelphia, Pennsylvania. (Some
Lutheran materials are also in the Library of the Lutheran Theological
Seminary at Gettysburg, Pennsylvania.) Many of the records of individual
congregations of these denominations, however, are in the archives of the
local churches and were consulted there.

Valuable information on American organ history has been collected
by the Organ Historical Society, an organization dedicated to the identification and preservation of the old "tracker action" organs. The Society pub-
lishes *The Tracker,* a periodical referred to frequently in these pages, and is
now establishing permanent archives at Ohio Wesleyan University.

WORKS RELATING DIRECTLY TO TANNENBERG

Beck, Abraham R., "David Tannenberg," *The Pennsylvania German,*
Vol. X, No. 7 (July, 1909), pp. 339-41.

Beck, Paul E., "David Tanneberger, Organ Builder," *Papers Read Before
the Lancaster County Historical Society,* Vol. XXX, No. 1 (1926),
pp. 3-11.

Church Music and Musical Life in Pennsylvania in the Eighteenth Century,
Vol. II. Philadelphia: Publications of the Pennsylvania Society of the
Colonial Dames of America, 1927.

Diffenderffer, F. R., "Some Historical Mistakes Corrected," *Papers Read
Before the Lancaster County Historical Society,* Vol. XXI, Nos. 8-9
(1917), pp. 143-44.

Genzmer, George Harvey, "David Tanneberger," *Dictionary of American
Biography,* XVIII. (New York: Charles Scribner's Sons, 1936),
294-95.

Hensel, W. U., "A Famous Organ Builder," *Papers Read Before the
Lancaster County Historical Society,* Vol. XI, No. 9 (1907), pp.
351-54.

Jordan, John W., "Early Colonial Organ-builders of Pennsylvania," *The
Pennsylvania Magazine of History and Biography,* XXII (1898),
231-33.

Knauss, James Owen, Jr., *Social Conditions Among the Pennsylvania
Germans in the 18th Century, as Revealed in the German Newspapers
Published in America.* Lancaster, Pa.: Vol. XXIX, Publications of
the Pennsylvania German Society, 1922.

Lob und Anbetung des Gottmenschen, am Tage der Einweihung der neuen

Orgel in der Deutschen Evangelisch Lutherischen Zions Kirche in Philadelphia, den 10 October, 1790. Germantaun, Pa.: Michael Billmeyer, 1790.

McCorkle, Donald M., "Prelude to a History of American Moravian Organs," *American Guild of Organists Quarterly,* Vol. III, No. 4 (October, 1958), pp. 142-48.

McCracken, Eugene E., "Pennsylvania, The Keystone State," *The Tracker,* Vol. IV, No. 2 (January, 1960), pp. 1, 3-4.

Schmauk, Theodore E., *The Church Organ and Its History.* Lebanon, Pa., n.d. Unpublished manuscript in the Archives of the Ministerium of Pennsylvania at the Lutheran Theological Seminary, Philadelphia, Pennsylvania.

Shields, T. Edgar, "Two Eighteenth-Century Organ Builders," *The American Organist,* Vol. 27, No. 6 (June, 1944), pp. 129-30.

Wolf, Edward C., "The Tannenberg Organ at Old Zion Church, Philadelphia," *Journal of Church Music,* Vol. 3, No. 4 (April, 1961), pp. 2-5.

TANNENBERG ORGAN RESTORATIONS

Eader, Thomas S., "David Tannenberg's Last Organ," *The Tracker,* Vol. IV, No. 3 (April, 1960), pp. 3-4.

McManis, Charles W., "David Tannenberg and the Old Salem Restoration," *The American Organist,* Vol. 48, No. 5 (May, 1965), pp. 15-20.

————, "Restoration of Tannenberg Organ at Old Salem," *The Diapason,* Vol. 56, No. 4 (March, 1965), pp. 36-37.

————, and Albright, Frank P., "Tannenberg Restoration," *The Tracker,* Vol. IX, No. 2 (Winter, 1965), pp. 1-2, 7-8.

"Organ of 1804 Restored," *The Diapason,* Vol. 51, No. 4 (March 1, 1960), p. 6.

"Tannenberg Organ Restored," *The American Organist,* Vol. 43, No. 5 (May, 1960), pp. 28-29.

ORGAN BUILDING

Audsley, George Ashdown, *The Art of Organ Building.* New York: Dodd, Mead, 1905. Two volumes.

Biggs, E. Power, "Welcome Back American Trackers," *The Diapason,* Vol. 51, No. 10 (September 1, 1960), pp. 18-19.

Broadhouse, John, *The Organ Viewed from Within.* London: William Reeves, n.d.

DeBrisay, A. C. Delacour, *The Organ and Its Music.* London: Kegan Paul, Trench, Trubner and Co., Ltd., 1934.

Joy, Charles R., *Music in the Life of Albert Schweitzer: With Selections from His Writings.* Boston: Beacon Paperback, 1959.

Schweitzer, Albert, *Out of My Life and Thought: An Autobiography.* New York: Mentor, 1955.

Sumner, William L., *The Organ: Its Evolution, Principles of Construction and Use,* third edition, revised and enlarged. London: MacDonald, 1962.

MORAVIAN MUSIC

Beck, Herbert H., "Lititz as an Early Musical Center," *Papers Read Before the Lancaster County Historical Society,* Vol. XIX, No. 3 (1915), pp. 71-81.

David, Hans Theo., "Musical Life in the Pennsylvania Settlements of the Unitas Fratrum," *Transactions of the Moravian Historical Society,* Vol. XIII, Part I (1942), pp. 19-58.

Finney, Theo. M., "The Collegium Musicum at Lititz, Pennsylvania, During the Eighteenth Century," *Papers Read by Members of the American Musicological Society* (1937).

Grider, Rufus A., *Historical Notes on Music in Bethlehem, Pennsylvania, from 1741-1871.* Philadelphia, 1873.

McCorkle, Donald M., "The Moravian Contribution to American Music," *Music Library Association Notes,* Vol. XIII, No. 4 (September, 1956), pp. 597-606.

————, *Moravian Music in Salem: A German-American Heritage.* Ann Arbor, Mich.: University Microfilms, Inc., 1958.

————, "Musical Instruments of the Moravians in North Carolina," *The American-German Review,* Vol. XXI, No. 3 (February-March, 1955), pp. 12-17.

Maurer, Joseph A., "Central Moravian Church: Center of Moravian Music," *The American Organist,* Vol. 41, No. 11 (November, 1958), pp. 407-12.

————,"The Moravian Trombone Choir," *Historical Review of Berks County,* Vol. XX, No. 1 (October-December, 1954), pp. 2-8.

"The Organs in Central Moravian Church," *The American Organist,* Vol. 41, No. 11 (November, 1958).

Rau, Albert G., and David, Hans T., *A Catalogue of Music by American Moravians, 1742-1842, from the Archives of the Moravian Church at Bethlehem, Pennsylvania.* Bethlehem: The Moravian Seminary and College for Women, 1938.

MORAVIAN HISTORY

Albright, S. C., *The Story of the Moravian Congregation at York, Penn-sylvania*. York: The Maple Press Co., Foreword dated 1927.

Barba, Preston A., *They Came to Emmaus: A History*. Emmaus, Pa.: Published by the Borough of Emmaus, 1959.

Bi-Centennial, the Moravian Church, Lebanon, Pennsylvania. 1947.

DeSchweinitz, Edmund, *The Life and Times of David Zeisberger*. Philadelphia: J. B. Lippincott and Co., 1870.

Fries, Adelaide L., *Customs and Practices of the Moravian Church*, revised edition. Winston-Salem, N. C.: Board of Christian Education and Evangelism [of the Moravian Church], 1964.

———— (ed.), *Records of the Moravians in North Carolina*, Vols. I-VII. Raleigh: North Carolina Historical Commission, 1922-47.

Hamilton, J. Taylor, "A History of the Church Known as the Moravian Church," *Transactions of the Moravian Historical Society*, Vol. VI.

Hamilton, Kenneth Gardiner, *John Ettwein and the Moravian Church During the Revolutionary Period*. Bethlehem, Pa.: Times Publishing Co., 1940.

Henry, James, "Christian's Spring," *Transactions of the Moravian Historical Society*, Vol. I, No. 2 (1857-58), pp. 64-77.

Jordan, John W., "Moravian Immigration to Pennsylvania, 1734-67," *Transactions of the Moravian Historical Society*, Vol. V, No. 2, pp. 51-90.

Levering, Joseph Mortimer, *A History of Bethlehem, Pennsylvania, 1741-1892*. Bethlehem: Times Publishing Co., 1903.

The Moravian Atlas. Fulneck [England]: By the Teachers of Fulneck Academy, 1853.

Myers, Elizabeth Lehman, *A Century of Moravian Sisters*. New York: Fleming H. Revell Co., 1918.

Neisser, Georg, *A History of the Beginnings of Moravian Work in America*. Bethlehem, Pa.: Publication No. 1 of the Archives of the Moravian Church, 1955.

————, "A List of the Bohemian and Moravian Emigrants to Saxony, Collected from Various Sources in Print and Manuscript; Begun and Completed at New York from June 2 to July 20, 1772," translated and edited by Albert G. Rau, *Transactions of the Moravian Historical Society*, Vol. IX, Nos. 1-2 (1913), pp. 37-93.

Nelson, Vernon H., *John Valentine Haidt*. Williamsburg, Va.: Abby Aldrich Rockefeller Folk Art Collection, 1966.

———— (ed.), and Fliegel, Carl John (trans.), *Christian David: Servant of the Lord*. Bethlehem, Pa.: Publications of the Archives of the

Moravian Church, Vol. II, 1962.

Oerter, A. L., "Graceham, Frederick County, Maryland, An Historical Sketch," *Transactions of the Moravian Historical Society,* Vol. IX, Nos. 3-4 (1913), pp. 119-305.

"A Petition by the Moravians During the Revolutionary War," *The Pennsylvania German,* Vol. XII, No. 1 (1911), pp. 43-45.

Reincke, Abraham, "A Register of the Members of the Moravian Church," *Transactions of the Moravian Historical Society,* Vol. I, Nos. 7-9 (1873), pp. 283-426.

Ritter, Abraham, *History of the Moravian Church in Philadelphia, From Its Foundation in 1742 to the Present Time.* Philadelphia: Hayes and Zell, 1857.

Schultze, Augustus, *Guide to the Old Moravian Cemetery of Bethlehem, Pennsylvania, 1742-1910.* Lancaster, Pa.: Pennsylvania German Society, Vol. XXI, 1910.

Spangenberg, August Gottlieb, *Leben des Herrn Nicolaus Ludwig Grafen und Herrn von Zinzendorf,* drei Bände. Zu finden in den Brüdergemeinen, 1772-74.

Two Centuries of Nazareth, 1740-1940. Nazareth, Pa.: Bi-Centennial, Inc., 1940.

Weinlick, John Rudolf, *Count Zinzendorf.* Nashville: Abingdon Press, 1956.

LITITZ

Beck, Abraham R., "Extracts from the Brethren's House and Congregational Diaries of the Moravian Church at Lititz, Pennsylvania, Relating to the Revolutionary War," *The Penn Germania,* Vol. I, Nos. 11-12 (November-December, 1912), pp. 849-62.

———, *"The Moravian Graveyards of Lititz, Pennsylvania, 1744-1905.* n.d.

Beck, Herbert H., "Graveyard of the Revolutionary Soldiers at Lititz," *Historical Papers and Addresses of the Lancaster County Historical Society,* XXXVII (1933), 1-5.

———, "The Military Hospital at Lititz, 1777-78," *Historical Papers and Addresses of the Lancaster County Historical Society,* Vol. XXIII, No. 1, pp. 5-14.

———, "Town Regulations of Lititz," *Historical Papers and Addresses of the Lancaster County Historical Society,* XXXIX (1935), 105-20.

Brickenstein, H. A., "Sketch of the Early History of Lititz, 1742-75," *Transactions of the Moravian Historical Society,* Vol. II, No. 7, pp. 343-74.

Zook, John G., *Historical and Pictorial Lititz.* Lititz, Pa.: Express Printing Co., 1905.

LOCAL HISTORIES

[Bachman, C. G.], *St. Stephen Reformed Church, New Holland, Pennsylvania.* 1951.

Beck, Clara A., "St. John's Lutheran Church, Centre Square," *Historical Sketches of the Historical Society of Montgomery County, Pennsylvania*, V, 52-72.

Berrian, William, *An Historical Sketch of Trinity Church, New York.* New York: Stanford and Swords, 1847.

Brong, W. H., "History of the Plainfield Church," *The Pennsylvania German*, Vol. X, No. 7 (July, 1909), pp. 305-17.

Cramer, W. Stuart, *History of the First Reformed Church, Lancaster, Pennsylvania, 1736-1904*, Vol. I. Lancaster: Wickersham Printing Co., 1904.

Dapp, Charles F., *History of Zion's or Old Organ Church.* Spring City, Pa.: The Inter-Borough Press, 1919.

DeLong, Calvin M., *Two Hundred Twenty-Five Years at New Goshenhoppen, 1727-1952.* Allentown, Pa.: Schlechter's, 1952.

Demme, C. R., *Zum Andenken an die hundertjährige Jubelfeier in der deutschen evangel. luther. St. Michaelis-Kirche in Philadelphia.* Philadelphia: Conrad Zentler, 1843.

Dix, Morgan (ed.), *A History of the Parish of Trinity Church in the City of New York*, Part I. New York: G. P. Putnam's Sons, 1898.

Dorr, Benjamin, *A Historical Account of Christ Church, Philadelphia.* Philadelphia: R. S. H. George, 1841.

Egle, William Henry, *History of the Counties of Dauphin and Lebanon.* Philadelphia: Everts and Peck, 1883.

Ellis, Franklin, and Evans, Samuel, *History of Lancaster County, Pennsylvania.* Philadelphia: Everts and Peck, 1883.

Eschbach, Edmund R., *Historic Sketch of the Evangelical Reformed Church of Frederick, Maryland.* 1894.

Fry, Jacob, *The History of Trinity Lutheran Church, Reading, Pennsylvania.* Reading: Published by the Congregation, 1894.

Gerhard, D. W., *A History of the New Holland Charge of the Reformed Church in Lancaster County, Pennsylvania.* New Holland: 1877.

Gibson, John (ed.), *History of York County, Pennsylvania.* Chicago: F. A. Battey Publishing Co., 1886.

Gilbert, D. M. (ed.), *Centennial of Zion Lutheran Church, Harrisburg.* Harrisburg, Pa.: Herr Publishing Co., 1896.

Hay, Ellis S., *One Hundred and Forty-Four Years: A Sketch of Emmanuel Reformed Church, Hanover, Pennsylvania, 1765-1909.*

Historical Discourse at the Sesqui-Centennial of Christ Evangelical Lutheran Church on the Tulpehocken near Stouchsburg, Berks County, Pennsylvania. Lebanon, Pa.: F. J. F. Schantz, 1894.

Huddle, W. P., *History of the Hebron Lutheran Church, Madison County, Virginia, from 1717 to 1907*. New Market, Va.: Henkel and Co., 1908.

Kershner, W. J., and Lerch, Adam G., *History of St. John's (Hain's) Reformed Church in Lower Heidelberg Township, Berks County, Pennsylvania*. Reading, Pa.: I. M. Beaver, 1916.

Kieffer, Henry Martyn, *Some of the First Settlers of "The Forks of the Delaware" and Their Descendents*. Easton, Pa., 1902.

Klein, H. M. J., and Diller, William F., *The History of St. James' Church (Protestant Episcopal) 1744-1944*. Lancaster, Pa.: Published by the Vestry, St. James' Church, 1944.

Kretschmann, Ernest T., *The Old Trappe Church*. Philadelphia: Published by the Congregation, 1893.

Lippold, John W., "Old Trinity Steeple," *Historical Papers and Addresses of the Lancaster County Historical Society,* Vol. XXXI, No. 9 (1927), pp. 127-33.

Mann, W. J., and Spaeth, A., *Fest-Gruss zum Zions-Jubiläum, Mai 13, 1866*. Philadelphia: C. W. Widmaier, 1866.

Matthews, Alfred, and Hungerford, Austin N., *History of the Counties of Lehigh and Carbon*. Philadelphia: Everts and Richards, 1884.

Messiter, A. H., *A History of the Choir and Music of Trinity Church, New York*. New York: Edwin S. Gorham, 1906.

Munsell, Joel, *The Annals of Albany,* second edition, Vol. I. Albany: Joel Munsell, 1869.

Prowell, George R., *History of York County, Pennsylvania,* Vol. II. Chicago: J. H. Beers and Co., 1907.

Ranck, James B., *et al., A History of the Evangelical Reformed Church, Frederick, Maryland*. 1964.

Roberts, Charles R., and Schindel, J. D., *History of Egypt Church*. Allentown, Pa.: Papers Read Before the Lehigh County Historical Society, 1908.

Schaeffer, C. F., and Muhlenberg, F. A., *Memorial Volume of the Evangelical Lutheran Church of the Holy Trinity, Lancaster, Pennsylvania*. Lancaster: John Baer's Sons, 1861.

Schmauk, Theodore E., *Old Salem in Lebanon*. Lebanon, Pa.: Congregation of Salem Evangelical Lutheran Church, 1898.

Sener, S. M., *The Catholic Church at Lancaster, Pennsylvania*. Philadelphia: American Catholic Historical Society, 1894.

Two Hundredth Anniversary, First Ziegel Church, 1750-1950. 1950.

Two Hundredth Anniversary of the Congregation [Zion-Moselem], *1734-1934*.

Wanner, J. D., *Kirchen-Recht der Zions Kirche ᴢⱼ Richmond, Berks County, Pennsylvania.* Kutztown, Pa.: "Geist der Zeit" Druckerei, 1863.

Wentz, Abdel Ross, *History of the Evangelical Lutheran Church of Frederick, Maryland, 1738-1938.* Harrisburg, Pa.: The Evangelical Press, 1938.

Worner, William Frederic, *Old Lancaster: Tales and Traditions.* Lancaster, Pa.: Published by the author, 1927.

Wust, Klaus G., *Zion in Baltimore, 1755-1955.* Baltimore: Zion Church of the City of Baltimore, 1955.

GENERAL

Anburey, Thomas, *Travels Through the Interior Parts of America,* Vol. II. Boston and New York: Houghton Mifflin Co., 1923.

"Ancient Home of Old Organ Builders," *The Pennsylvania German,* Vol. X, No. 4 (1909), pp. 174-75.

Berky, Andrew S. (ed.), *The Journals and Papers of David Schultze,* Vol. I. Pennsburg, Pa.: The Schwenkfelder Library, 1952.

Blumer, George, "Dr. William Brown," *Dictionary of American Biography,* Vol. III. New York: Charles Scribner's Sons, 1929.

Brecht, Samuel Kriebel, *The Genealogical Record of the Schwenkfelder Families.* New York: Rand McNally Co., 1923.

[Brown, William], *Pharmacopoeia Simpliciorum et Efficaciorum, in usum nosocomii militaris, ad exercitum Foederatarum Americae Civitatum pertinentis; Hodiernae nostrae inopiae rerumque angustiis, Feroci hostium saevitiae, belloque crudeli ex inopinato patriae nostrae illato debitis, Maxime accommodata.* Philadelphia: Ex officina Styner and Cist, 1778.

Butterfield, L. H. (ed.), *Adams Family Correspondence,* Vol. II. Cambridge, Mass.: Belknap Press of Harvard University Press, 1963.

Drummond, R. R., *Early German Music in Philadelphia.* New York: D. Appleton and Co., 1910.

Dubbs, Joseph Henry, "Formative Influences," *The College Student,* March, 1908. Publication of Franklin and Marshall College, Lancaster, Pa.

Eberlein, Harold Donaldson and Hubbard, Cortland Van Dyke, "Music in the Early Federal Era," *The Pennsylvania Magazine of History and Biography,* LXIX (1945), 103-27.

Eckhardt, George H., *Pennsylvania Clocks and Clockmakers.* New York: Devin-Adair Co., 1955.

Fitzpatrick, John C. (ed.), *The Diaries of George Washington,* Vol. IV. Boston and New York: Houghton Mifflin Co., 1925.

Franklin, Benjamin, *The Autobiography of Benjamin Franklin*. New Haven: Yale University Press, 1964.

Gahn, Bessie W., "Dr. William Brown, Physician-General to the American Army," *Journal of the American Pharmaceutical Association*, Vol. XVI, No. 11 (November, 1927), pp. 1090-91.

Gerhard, E. S. (ed.), *Schwenkfelder Craftsmen, Inventors and Surveyors,* Schwenkfeldiana, Vol. I, No. 5. Norristown, Pa.: Board of Publication of the Schwenkfelder Church, 1945.

Green, Jack (ed.), *The Diary of Colonel Landon Carter*, Vol I. Charlottesville, Va.: The University Press of Virginia, 1965.

Guthrie, William, *A New System of Modern Geography*, Vol. II. Philadelphia: Printed for Matthew Carey, 1795.

Heiges, George L., *Henry William Stiegel and His Associates*. Lancaster, Pa.: Rudisill and Co., Inc., 1948.

Journals of the House of Representatives of the Commonwealth of Pennsylvania, November 28, 1776-October 2, 1781, Vol. I. Philadelphia: John Dunlap, 1782.

Kipling, Rudyard, *Rewards and Fairies*. London: Macmillan and Co., Ltd., 1914.

Kistler, William U., "Early Organ Builders in Northern Montgomery County," *Historical Sketches of the Historical Society of Montgomery County, Pennsylvania*, IV (1910), 112-17.

McCracken, Eugene M., "Duck Soup," *The Tracker*, Vol. IV, No. 1 (October, 1959), pp. 9-12, and No. 2 (January, 1960), pp. 11-12.

———, "The Spirits Cost $0.75," *The Tracker*, Vol. V, No. 2 (January, 1961), pp. 6-8.

Mencken, H. L., *The American Language, Supplement I*. New York: Alfred A. Knopf, 1962.

Mereness, Newton D., *Travels in the American Colonies*. New York: Antiquarian Press, Ltd., 1961.

Montgomery, Thomas Lynch (ed.), *Pennsylvania Archives,* Fifth Series, Vol. VII. Harrisburg, Pa.: Harrisburg, Publishing Co., State Printer, 1906.

"Narrative of the Journey of the Schwenkfelders to Pennsylvania, 1733," *The Pennsylvania Magazine of History and Biography*, X (1886), 167-79.

Ogden, John C., *An Excursion into Bethlehem and Nazareth in Pennsylvania in the Year 1799*. Philadelphia: Printed by Charles Cist, 1805.

"An Organ of 1819: Built by Philip Bachman," *The American Organist,* Vol. 16, No. 5 (May, 1933), p. 262.

Parsons, Jacob Cox (ed.), *Extracts from the Diary of Jacob Hiltzheimer of Philadelphia, 1765-98*. Philadelphia: William F. Fell and Co., 1893.

Strassburger, Ralph B., and Hinke, William J., *Pennsylvania German Pioneers,* 3 vols. Norristown, Pa.: Pennsylvania German Society, 1934.
Wittke, Carl, *We Who Built America: The Saga of the Immigrant.* Cleveland: The Press of Western Reserve University, 1939.

DISCOGRAPHY

Arias, Anthems and Chorales of the American Moravians, Vol. I. The Moravian Festival Chorus and Orchestra under Thor Johnson. Columbia Records: ML 5427, MS 6102.
Arias, Anthems and Chorales of the American Moravians, Vol. II. The Moravian Festival Chorus and Orchestra under Thor Johnson. Columbia Records: ML 5688, MS 6288.
The Chorale Prelude, George Weckman, Organist, with the Choir of the Lutheran Theological Seminary at Philadelphia. In part recorded on the 1791 Tannenberg organ at Zion Lutheran Church, Spring City, Pennsylvania. Monophonic MA 6, Ken-Del Productions, Inc., Wilmington, Delaware, 1963.
John Antes, *Three Trios: The Birth of Chamber Music in America.* Performed by members of the Fine Arts Quartet. Music of the American Moravians, Vol. III, Columbia Records: ML 6141, MS 6741.
The Organ, An Aural and Visual Guide Complied and Discussed by E. Power Biggs, With the Sounds of Many Modern and Historic Organs. Columbia Records: DL 5288.
The Organ in America. Performed by E. Power Biggs. Substantial portions of this record are played on the 1804 Tannenberg organ at York, Pennsylvania. Columbia Records: ML 5496, MS 6161.

INDEX